*Portrait of the Rev. Dr. Florence Li Tim-Oi on her eightieth birthday.*

*Tenth anniversary of the ordination of women priests with five clergy from the Diocese of Hong Kong and Macau, 1981. Left to right, the Rev. Mary Au, the Rev. Joyce Bennett, the Rev. Florence Li, the Rev. Jane Huang, the Rev. Wing Shue Sek.*

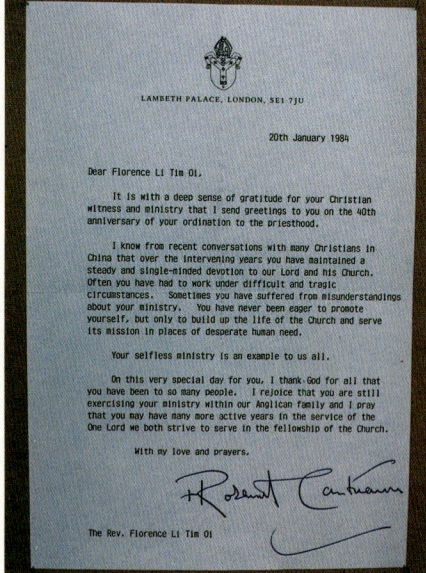

*Congratulatory letter from Archbishop Robert Runcie to Florence Li on the fortieth anniversary of her ordination to the priesthood, 1984. It was read at the Westminster Abbey celebration.*

*Pilgrimage to the Holy Land, 1985. First row from left, Florence and her sister Rita Lee.*

*Florence and the Rev. Joyce Bennett visit Fortrose Cathedral, Inverness, Scotland, in 1986.*

*Eightieth birthday celebration procession, 1987.*

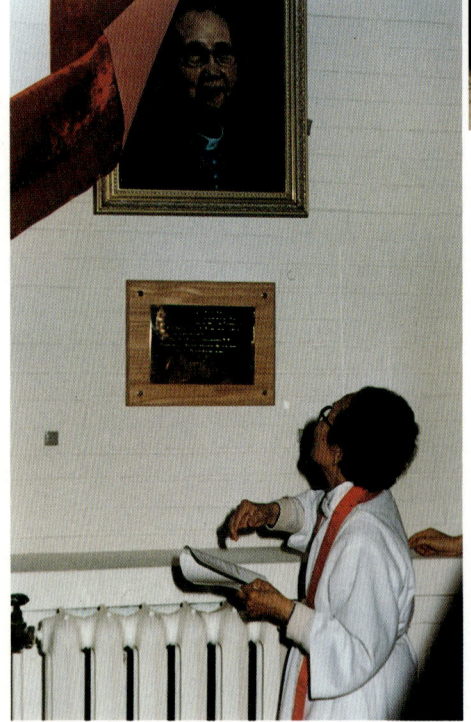

*Unveiling her own portrait and the plaque of the Li Tim-Oi church hall.*

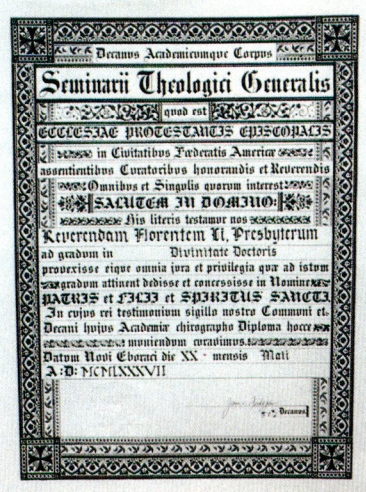

*Awarded Doctor of Divinity, General Theological Seminary, New York, 1987. Diploma (top) with the dignitaries (bottom).*

*Florence with Archbishop Robert Runcie, 1988, Lambeth.*

*Florence with brother-in-law Siu Ting Chui, sister Rita Lee, and Mrs. Emily Wong, a member of St John's Anglican Church, Toronto.*

*Awarded Doctor of Divinity by Trinity College, University of Toronto, 1991.*

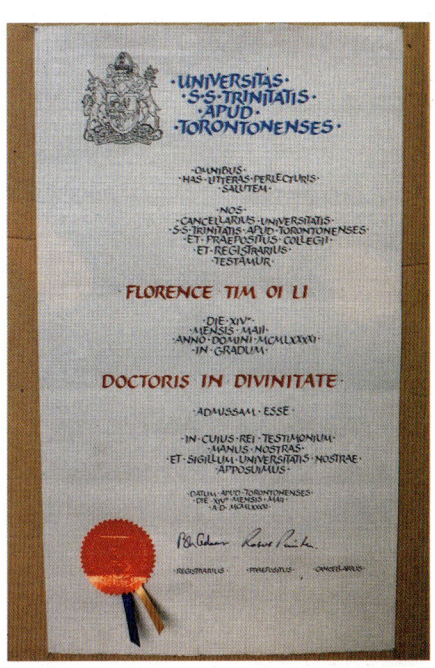

*Florence with sister Rita Lee-Chui, chief donor of the Li Tim-Oi Foundation, London, England.*

# Raindrops of My Life

# Raindrops of My Life

Memoirs of the
Reverend Florence Li Tim-Oi

**Anglican Book Centre**
**Toronto, Canada**

1996
Anglican Book Centre
600 Jarvis Street
Toronto, Ontario
Canada M4Y 2J6

Copyright © by Anglican Book Centre

All rights reserved. No part of this book may be reproduced, stored in a retrieval system, or transmitted, in any form, or by any means, electronic, mechanical, photocopying, recording, or otherwise, without the written permission of the Book Centre.

Publication of this book has been assisted by grants from The Anglican Foundation, the Li Tim-Oi Foundation in London, England, and St John's Chinese Congregation, Anglican, in Toronto.

Note: All biblical quotations are from the *New International Version*.

**Canadian Cataloguing in Publication Data**

Li, Florence Tim Oi, 1907–
    Raindrops of my life

ISBN 1-55126-128-6

1. Li, Florence Tim Oi, 1907–   2. China – History – 20th century.   3. Women priests – China – Biography.   4. Anglican Communion – China – Clergy – Biography.   I. Title.

BX5680.L5A3   1995      283'.092      C95-9330755-5

# Contents

Foreword
    *The Reverend Canon Edmund B. Der*   vii
Chronology of the Christian Church in China after 1949   ix
Synopsis of Political Development in China, 1949–1980   xii
Preface   xvii

**Part One: 1907–1944**
1. South Corner   1
2. Loving Parents   2
3. Further Education in Hong Kong   5
4. The Process of My Calling   7
5. Theological Training   9
6. Field Placement at All Saints' Church, Kowloon   11
7. Transfer to Macau   12
8. Grateful and Unforgettable   17
9. Braving Danger to Save My Father   18
10. Ordination to Priesthood   20
11. The Controversy over Ordaining Women   22
12. Establishing a Permanent Base in Macau   23

**Part Two: 1947–1980**
13. Reminiscences of Hepu   25
14. Further Studies in Beijing   28
15. Back to Guangzhou   30
16. A Facade of Peace and Prosperity   34
17. Learning from the School of Socialism   35
18. Joining the History Writing Group   36
19. The Movement of the Red Guards   37
20. The Cleansing Movement   39
21. Retirement from the Factory   43
22. My Financial Situation   45
23. Religious Freedom Restored   45

**Part Three: 1981–1985**
24. My Application to Visit Relatives Abroad   48
25. My Stay in Hong Kong   48

26. Activities Abroad    49
27. Settling Down in Toronto    50
28. The Fortieth Ordination Anniversary Celebration in Toronto    51
29. The Celebration in England    53
30. Travelling to Geneva, Rome, and Paris    58
31. Back to Toronto    60
32. Joining a Pilgrimage to Jerusalem    61
33. Another Journey to Europe    63
34. Revisiting England    65

**Part Four: 1985–1992**
35. Moving to a New Home    67
36. Joining the Activities of Toronto Churches    67
37. 1986 Canterbury Pilgrimage and Joining Hands Conference    68
38. In Memory of the Late Bishop Gilbert Baker of Hong Kong    69
39. Attending the Tenth Anniversary Celebration of the Ordination of Women to Priesthood in the Anglican Church of Canada    69
40. My Trip to China    71
41. A Happy Birthday and Receiving My Degree    77
42. A Special Guest of the Lambeth Conference    79
43. The Consecration of the Rev. Barbara Harris    81
44. A Pacific Cruise    82
45. Reflections during Convalescence    83
46. Receiving My Second Honour    85

In Remembrance of My Sister, Tim-Oi
    *Rita K. Lee-Chui*    87
A Sermon Preached on the Golden Anniversary of the Ordination of Florence Li Tim-Oi
    *Archbishop Ted Scott*    91
Thoughts at the First Ordination of Women Priests at Oxfordshire
    *Christopher Hall*    97
A Sermon Preached on the Golden Jubilee of the Ordination of Florence Li Tim-Oi
    *Archbishop Donald Coggan*    100

# *Foreword*

In my thirty years of priesthood, I was most helped and moved by my team ministry with the Rev. Florence Li Tim-Oi. This world famous and experienced pastor listened attentively and gave me able assistance and encouragement. In her convalescence following an injury to her lower back, Florence was bed-ridden for seven months. She gave our parishioners an opportunity to learn how to serve and nurse a patient with integrity and care.

Her endurance and persistence were exemplary; she was always a pilgrim running towards the Cross of Jesus. Despite changes of title, honour, or pastoral role, she endured all with thanksgiving and a praiseful heart, never mindful of favour or disgrace. She was different from feminist activists in that she moved and convinced others through her humble, gentle, feminine piety.

She might only have been a minor character in the eight-year Sino-Japanese war, but her faithfulness and dedication in her labour along with Jesus won her the respect and love of many. Arranging the requiem of the Rev. Li was a new experience for me. It drew many people from very different perspectives. Cables of condolences for this contemporary saint of ours came from all over the world.

The memoirs of Florence Li Tim-Oi will take many of us into an unfamiliar time and space. Reading her story may seem like entering the maze of an ancient Chinese mandarin's garden in Soochow, with winding paths, bridges, and tunnels amidst a man-made mountain. Yet, these memoirs offer us a taste of China and the experience of the brave Christians who lived through the turbulent times of revolution, the Sino-Japanese war, the Liberation war, and the aftermath of class struggles and social revisions.

At the peak of these movements, Florence was totally involved and was, no doubt, one of the leaders riding the wave. It might appear that Florence was unduly influenced by the ideology of socialism. In fact, she was apolitical and maintained her Christian realism throughout. In some passages, she seems to extol the achievements of the Chinese Communists, having lived long enough to compare the accomplishments of various regimes. She was not a social critic, however, and it was in her good nature to appreciate the better side of humanity.

Florence titled her memoirs *The Raindrops of My Life*, because she wrote them from memory rather than from notes (all of her records prior to 1945 were destroyed in a fire). For that reason, there may be minor discrepancies in her account of her life and ministry. What is amazing is that her memories are so detailed. Her alertness and sensitivity are remarkable when one considers how we ourselves might have fared living through war, revolutions, and a labour camp experience.

With patience and a pilgrim's heart, let us proceed to study this adventurous account of her faith and ministry.

I wish to thank my associate, the Rev. Dr. Dean Mercer for editing the English version. We owe Mr. Gabriel W.K. Wong a thank you for his research for the synopsis of political development in China. May the Lord use the book to call many more servants for His vineyard.

*The Reverend Canon Edmund B. Der,*
*Rector of St Matthew's and St John's parish, Toronto*

# A Brief Chronology of the Christian Church in China after 1949
*(based on interviews with Chinese leaders in China, 1994)*

*1949*      The establishment of the People's Republic of China; Church life continued as usual.

*1950–1951*      Korean War broke out. Foreign missionaries were suspected of being foreign agents and were asked to leave. The whole nation was caught up in anti-American sentiment in aid of Korea. One hundred and fifty Protestant leaders met and voted to sever ties with foreign missions.

*1952*      Land reforms in the rural area. Rural churches ceased to function but urban churches carried on. "Three-anti's" and "five-anti's" seriously affected individual Christians and land owners and shop owners. Twelve seminaries of East China were combined and re-established at Jing Ling Theological College in Nanjing.

*1954*      The first National Christian Council met in Beijing and Mr. Y. T. Wu, YMCA secretary, led the establishment of the Three-Self Patriotic Movement (self-administration, self support, self-propagating). He secured 400,000 signatories to support the 232 delegates representing the sixty-two Protestant organizations and churches, now joined. K. H. Ting, an Anglican priest, became General Secretary of Kwong Shieh Huai—The Christian Society for Promoting Knowledge.

*1955*      K. H. Ting was consecrated Bishop of Zhejian Diocese.

*1957*      During an anti-rightist movement, pastors were labelled as rightists, and same as the educated and intellectuals. The Church was restricted. The Catholics founded the Chinese

| | |
|---|---|
| | Patriotic Catholic Association and the Orthodox Church founded a similar organization. |
| *1958* | The Great Leap Forward, a massive industrial and agricultural revolution designed to catch up with the West, was implemented. Communes were set up. City congregations were ordered to amalgamate. Hangzhau's nineteen churches were combined into five. Young pastors were forced to take up labour work as pastors had been labelled persecutors and parasites. |
| *1958–1965* | The Three-Self Patriotic Movement became active in liaising with the government. Churches were diminishing. The anti-rightist movement became more belligerent against the Church. Retracting from faith and Church membership was hailed as heroic, and "religionless" areas were declared. An extreme leftist revolution took the lead. |
| *1964* | In Guangzhou, special areas had enforced study classes to persuade Christians to recant their faith and withdraw their membership. Any overseas links were suspect. Among the Roman Catholics in Shanshi, Northeast China, and Zhejian, mass meetings were held where people recanted their faith. |
| *1966–1981* | The Cultural Revolution erupted. Religious books and artifacts were burned. Churches were closed, but many Christians met secretly in homes. Ministers were sent to communes for farming or into factories to work. Some area churches formed their own factories. |
| *1979–1991* | Churches were permitted to re-open and all Church activities slowly revived. Tung Shan Church in Guangzhou and Hangzhou were re-opened. Negotiations were started to retrieve Church property. Some were rented out to pay for the ministers and back-pay all salaries. The Third National Council met. Bishop K. H. Ting was elected chairman. |
| *1981* | Seminaries were opened, with courses for short-term training of evangelists, two-year to four-year training for pastors, as well as the opening of Jing Ling Theological College as a post-graduate school. Twelve schools are now open. |

## Problems in the Church in China

Great numbers have joined the Church and many new churches or meeting points have been started. The shortage of adequately trained clergy is quite severe. Government policy does not endorse foreign missionaries. The ministerial order is maintained in bishops (non-territorial), pastors, teachers, evangelists, and elders.

## The Attitude of the Chinese Communists towards Religion

Communist Party directives do not show a high regard for religion. While giving religious beliefs low priority, they tolerate religious faiths in general.

Each of the constitutions written and adopted by the Chinese government since the Communists came to power include an article on religious freedom (1954, 1975, 1978). Article 46 reads:

> Citizens enjoy freedom to believe in religion and freedom not to believe in religion and to propagate atheism.

In June 1981, the Sixth Plenary Session of the eleventh Central Committee of the Chinese Communist Party resolved that

> religious believers must not engage in propaganda against Marxism-Leninism and Mao Zedong Thought, and ... must not interfere with politics and education in their religious activities.

In 1982, a new section on religious freedom was written:

> Citizens of the People's Republic of China enjoy freedom of religious belief. No state organ, public organization or individual may compel citizens to believe in, or not to believe in, any religion. The state protects normal religious activities.... Religious bodies and religious affairs are not subject to any foreign domination.

There are now only two Anglican bishops still alive in China. Since the Cultural Revolution, all denominations have disappeared, to be replaced by the China Christian Council (Chair, Bishop Ting) which, together with local Christian Councils, represents the whole structure of Protestant Christianity. Two new bishops, elected by the Council without diocesan jurisdiction, represent their church and act as moral examples to the faithful.

# Synopsis of Political Development in China, 1949–1980

## 1949–1952: A Period of Mass Campaigns

After the defeat of Japan in 1945 the corruption and inability to rule of the Nationalist Government under Chiang Kai Shek led to civil war and a general loss of morale. Mao Zedong and the Chinese Communist Party led a Common Front alliance which came to power in China in October 1949. Against such a backdrop, the agenda for the Communists was simple, but onerous—to consolidate and take control of the entire nation.

As revolutionaries, it would therefore not be surprising for the new rulers to practice mass upheavals to achieve their purposes. Campaigns were thus utilized to unite the people's power to overthrow injustice and bring about changes.

### *Land Reform*

Land reforms were instigated between 1948 and 1952 to change the pattern of ownership and eliminate the landlords and rich peasant classes. Mass meetings were organized with public denunciation of "bad elements," while peasants were encouraged to speak out against injustices suffered. However, as the campaign picked up momentum, it became bloodier and more violent.

### *Marriage Law*

Between 1950 and 1953, campaigns were launched under the blessings of Mao to implement women's liberation and a "new democratic" form of marriage. One motive for these reforms was to weaken the grip of the family and clan systems, freeing the individual to participate in society as a whole.

## Suppression of Counter-Revolutionaries

Under a purely political agenda to strike against "internal enemies," large numbers were purged in the year of 1951. During this period, waves of arrests and mass trials were conducted throughout the country. This was often referred to as the ominous "reign of terror."

## Thought Reform

With Mao's wife Jian Qing pioneering the criticism against intellectuals or idealistic reformers, many well-known writers were forced into self-criticism and public confessions. In an all-out effort to achieve conformity and conversion, the education system, including its educators and teachers, was subjected to an intensive thought-control campaign that lasted into 1952.

# 1953–1957: Socialist Transformation

From 1953 to 1957, China focused on social development. However, as was not uncommon with China's policies, results were uneven and often met with compromise in direction and execution.

## First Five-Year Plan

In preparing the way for socialism, emphasis was placed on "heavy industry." In agriculture, peasants were organized and Agricultural Co-operatives (APC's) were formed. Growth, however, was sluggish and harvest, dismal.

## High Tide

By 1955, the non-performance and ultimate dissolution of the APC's had dismayed Mao. In return, Mao mobilized his own support by gathering provincial and sub-provincial Party secretaries, and called for a "High Tide" of Socialist transformation. By conducting a vigorous campaign to complete collectivization, both the countryside and cities were taken over or organized into cooperatives.

## Hundred Flowers Campaign

Prior to 1956, tension was evident between the people and the Party. By advocating his thinking, "Let a Hundred Flowers Bloom, Let a Hundred Schools of Thought Contend" and "Long-Term co-existence and Mutual Supervision," Mao turned towards Party rectification and accepted criticism against the Party from non-Communists. As criticism mounted, however, Mao reacted with renewed repression against the intellectuals.

## 1958–1960: The Great Leap Forward

With the advent of industrial and agricultural growth, social revolution, and the desire to achieve pre-set goals simultaneously, China necessitated an all-out mobilization. Thus an outburst of events, collectively known as the Great Leap Forward, followed on an unprecedented scale. These included the mobilization of ninety million people to learn steel making, the migration of twenty million peasants, and a campaign to eliminate the "Four Pests."

Mighty and elaborate as it seemed, the Great Leap Forward failed considerably as a modernizing effort. While it caused economic setbacks, soured foreign relations, and opened serious political wounds, it also plunged China into hunger, unemployment, and lawlessness.

## 1960–1965: Depression, Recovery, and Adjustment

By 1961, China had reached a nadir of hardship and suffering. Beginning in 1962, however, a glimmer of hope started to emerge.

In February 1962, the Great Leap Forward was abandoned. It was also during this period that Deng Xiao Ping started to gain prominence. His efforts to extend private plots, free markets, and reliance on private enterprises led China out of its depression.

In 1965, however, there were disagreements among Party officials over a wide variety of subjects. The political manoeuvres that followed subsequently led to the Great Proletarian Cultural Revolution.

## 1966–1969: The Great Proletarian Cultural Revolution

In brief, the Cultural Revolution was a power struggle and fight over ideological differences initiated by Mao as his own personal revolution.

During the months of May to July 1966, Mao was pushing for a cultural renewal. In heeding the warnings that representatives of the bourgeoisie had sneaked into the Party, Maoist factions urged high schools, universities, and radical students to carry out the Great Proletarian Cultural Revolution. The intense criticism of Party leaders and administrators was thus unleashed.

In August 1966, Mao used the designation of "Red Guards" for his new recruits and praised them for their actions. And, for the first time, the slogan "Rebellion is Justified" was used.

The Movement took on a violent and harsh turn. Bands of young rowdies burst into homes and confiscated Western artefacts. Intellectuals were subjected to verbal and physical abuse, and many died as a result of torture. In addition, monuments, gravestones, and even temples were defaced and destroyed.

At the same time, workers, People's Liberation Army personnel, and ex-students had formed their own revolutionary associations. China had become a hot-pot of violence, uncontrollable and destructive.

A brief moderation occurred in January 1967, but was subsumed by further mayhem and chaos in July and August. Finally, in September 1967, Mao recanted his original faith in the students and imposed military order. Order began to return in the summer of 1968.

## 1970–1980: The Aftermath

In the wake of upheaval in China was a "Lost Generation" of Red Guards and radicals who had out-lived their original praise from Chairman Mao. They were ultimately expended when things went out of control.

"Moderates" began to take control of the political front as the Chinese nation was sick and tired of unreasonable intrusion into their private lives. Meanwhile, an un-Maoist approach was adopted to modernize China amidst the rubble and lost morale.

Beginning in 1977, Deng Xiao Ping became the champion of popular policies, and the economy as cultural liberalization and openness to the outside was promoted.

GUANDONG PROVINCE

# *Preface*

In the twinkling of an eye, white sideburns portend the evening of my life. I appreciate and exclaim the Chinese proverb, "The gloaming is golden, yet the better is still in the morrow."

These words encouraged me and motivated me, not so much to re-embark on a trek of glory, but to be willing to become like a child, to learn from agile eagles to spread my wings and soar through the clouds and view the beautiful land created by God.

So I reminisce now about the pitter-patter of events, the raindrops of my life, as a living testimony to the Creator.

You drench its furrows
and level its ridges;
you soften it with showers
and bless its crops.
You crown the year with your bounty,
and your carts overflow with abundance.
The grasslands of the desert overflow;
the hills are clothed with gladness.
The meadows are covered with flocks
and the valleys are mantled with grain;
they shout for joy and sing.

*Psalm 65:10–13*

# Part 1
# *1907–1946*

✜ ✜ ✜

## 1. South Corner

South Corner is the world of my earliest memories. It is where loving my neighbours, loving the arts, and the habit of diligence were nurtured in me. South Corner was the living quarters assigned by my father to me and my sisters. I called it "Transcendence." From the name, it is apparent that my innocent young mind was already focused away from the secular world.

I was interested in needlework. I embroidered flowers, butterflies, and birds with multi-coloured silk threads. I crocheted and knitted. As I was more adept than other village girls, many young ladies came to learn my craft. As many as ten tailors in Yuen Long, Hong Kong, had contracts with me for final embroidery work. Moreover, a number of my wealthy lady friends' wedding pillow cases were the gifts of my painstaking needlecraft.

After graduating from the Yuen Long Government School at age fourteen, I had to stay at home for a while. My brothers had gone on to study in Hong Kong, and my father's limited salary did not permit all of his eight children to receive a higher education at the same time. However, sexual inequality did not prevail in our household, and I was adamantly opposed to the Chinese dictum, "Ignorance in female means Virtue."

During the next six years, I became a volunteer teacher of the Chinese and English Fundamental Curriculum. There were many neighbourhood girls whose parents lived overseas, and in order to reunite with them, the girls needed to learn basic conversational English. I was glad to help them in this way. During the same period, I helped my mother take care of my younger siblings.

Learning to love my neighbours and the arts and to be diligent at a tender age was in accordance with God's demands on His children. Jesus said, "Of all commandments, the greatest are to love God and to love your neighbour as yourself." When God first created the world, He lovingly said to His every handiwork, "God saw that it was good" (Gen. 1:10). God appreciates beauty. The psalmist wrote: "When I consider your heavens / The work of your fingers / The moon and the stars / which you have set in place..." (Psalm 8:3).

God delights in beautifying the world and everything in it. As God created humans in His image, and breathed life into them and made them ruler over all creatures, loving other people is part of loving God. God wants us to have beautiful lives. "He awaits us to reflect His glory" (Psa. 19:1).

## 2. Loving Parents

I was born on the fifth of May, 1907, in Shek Pai Bay, Aberdeen, of Hong Kong. My grandfather was from South Sea County of Guangdong Province but my father had been born in Fujien Province. In his youth, my father followed my grandfather in and out of the Hong Kong Governor's House. That was because my grandfather was the executive chef for the early governors of Hong Kong around the terms of Sir Hercules George Robert Robinson and Sir George Ferguson Bowen (1862-1885). Father went to Queen's College to study English and passed his exams. He then entered Hong Kong Government Hospital to read Medicine. He often told me proudly that Dr. Sun Yat-Sen was his classmate in medical school, in the same residence, the same room. He often took out a thick medical textbook and showed me the autograph of his professor. He spoke of how this Professor Cantlie had rescued Dr. Sun Yat-Sen from prison in London and jeopardized the Manchu Dynasty's scheme to quash the Revolution.

Dr. Sun Yat-Sen tried many times to convince my father to join the Revolution to overthrow the Manchu Dynasty. However, father declined every time, as he was convinced that bloodshed was unavoidable in a revolution. He did not wish to risk sacrificing himself for this cause as he was the only male to carry on the "lamp of incense"—the lineage of, not only his father, but all his uncles. Father's feudal upbringing overshadowed his revolutionary spirit. In his heart, educating his children to responsibly contribute to society was the proper form of patriotism.

Father trained in medicine at Ho Mui-Ling Hospital in Hong Kong. He then followed the Rev. Li Shu-Kwai of the Chinese Christian Church to Hua County Tsenei Village to practice there. However, Western medicine was not popular then, and so he took examinations to become a principal of the Hong Kong Public Schools system. This allowed him to earn a steady income and raise his children. Fortunately, God arranged this way out for him at his time of trial, and his faith moved forward as a result.

Father served as principal of the Government English Primary School in the area. When I was five, Father was transferred to Ping Shan in the western part of the New Territories. Shortly after this, the school moved about two miles north to Yuen Long. In 1932, Father endeavoured to build new premises on the slopes of Autau. He was principal of the school for over thirty years. Father enjoyed being at home after work each day and seldom ventured out. He loved to read both local and foreign books and magazines. He became very informed about world affairs without ever stepping outside his front door. People from all walks of life came to chat with him or to solicit his help when settling disputes in the village.

Father originally belonged to the Hong Kong Baptist Church but transferred to the Chinese Christian Church Yuen Long Parish when we moved to Yuen Long, since it was nearby. Under the leadership of Mr. Wong Shut-Fong, it was very active and vibrant. Father was on the board of directors and was treasurer. However, when my brother Ching-Yiu went to St. Paul's Boys' College to study and was baptised at St Paul's Church of Glenealy, most of our siblings joined that parish. Subsequently, our parents followed us there to worship in the Anglican Church.

My mother was my mentor in Chinese culture. She used the three-volumed "Red Book" of Chinese classics as her text. The only daughter of her parents, she was truly a "pearl in the palm." Even though she was born of a fisherman's family bound by feudal thought, she attended a Catholic convent school for six months and there learned colourful embroidery techniques. Her embroidery specialities were vivid roosters, birds, gay flowers, green pines, and emerald bamboo. Sadly, though, her desire to be a housewife was destroyed when a fortune-teller advised her that she should never marry to be the first wife, but must "sit aside." In other words, she had to be a concubine in order to bring blessings and prosperity to her husband and children.

I remember a delightful incident concerning my mother. She kept a pig, and fed it from a suckling until it grew to a total of eighty catties (about 110 pounds). Then, for father's birthday celebration, she had the pig sent to a barbecue shop to be roasted. When her children came home from summer vacation, they could enjoy (in Chinese terminology) the "natural order" of happy family life.

My father's first wife died of colon cancer in her later years and my half-brothers and half-sister were all cared for and nurtured by my mother. Taking care of eight children was not a light responsibility. However, although my mother had received little education, she was clever. She was insightful and analytical, diligent and frugal, and she managed the household adeptly.

My maternal grandparents were idol worshippers. Since my mother was their only daughter, she felt that she had to wait till they had passed away before she could be baptized, even though she possessed a strong faith long before. She loved to recite Jesus' teaching: "Come to me, all you who are weary and heavily laden, and I will give you rest. Take my yoke upon you and learn from me, for I am gentle and humble in heart, and you will find rest for your souls" (Matt. 11:28,29). Faith is strength. Leaning on God's strength, my mother could happily provide five of my brothers with all the material and spiritual support they needed to attend university. She treated all eight of us equally, encouraging us to study hard and be capable in order to serve our society. All of us revered our mother's love, kindness, and thoughtfulness.

In his later years, my father proudly wrote a poem to glorify my mother's contribution to our family and his satisfaction in her having raised his children responsibly:

> Worthy to be called a wife of noble character and a good mother,
> the Family prospers on her diligence and endurance;
> Ching-Yiu attained his Medical Doctorate,
> For ten years practices in Guangzhou.
> Tim-Oi (Florence) is a Professor at Canton Union Theological College,
> Spreading her name while spreading God's way;
> Kwei-King (Rita) travelled to England to get her Masters,
> What an honour it is for her to work for the International Labour Office.
> Ping, Ying, Kwai-Cheung travelled to Jamaica,
> They ran successful businesses during the War;
> Chung-Yiu, Hon-Yiu got their Bachelors degrees,
> Working hard for years to build up their families;

I am almost an octogenarian now,
Contented in my seniority with my grandchildren around me, tranquil and happy;
Still I hope my children will do their best,
Success lofty as a hundred feet pole but still forward advance.

Father passed away in 1954. No matter how hard I tried, I could not get permission to leave Guangzhou to attend his funeral, due to the strict control of the movements of all citizens. Bishop Hall personally attended All Saints' Church in Kowloon to officiate the funeral service. My father in heaven and all of my family were very grateful for the Bishop's graciousness.

My mother died on April 1, 1959. The first time that I was able to place flowers on the graves of my parents was when I went back to Hong Kong in 1987. Their faces in the picture on the tombstone seemed to smile sweetly on me, and I could almost hear them say, "We are face to face at last!" The writer of Revelations wrote, "Blessed are the dead who die in the Lord from now on. 'Yes,' says the Spirit, 'they will rest from their labour, for their deeds will follow them'" (Rev. 14:13).

## 3. Further Education in Hong Kong

Since my father's salary was meagre, my parents scrimped and saved but were only able to send the older boys to secondary school in Hong Kong and then on to university. In my private prayers, my own further education was first on the list of supplications. "The Spirit intercedes for the saints in accordance with God's will" (Rom. 8:27). God "is able to do immeasurably more than we ask or imagine, according to his power that is at work within us" (Eph. 3:20). From God's Word, I received much enlightenment and comfort, and my dream actually came true. It was another witness that God listens to the prayers of His children. I waited six years for the wonderful will of God, and learned that patience is an indispensable virtue in life.

There was a great general strike in Hong Kong in 1925. Labour gained unprecedented victory, and all Chinese public servants were given salary increases. Father received a huge, lump-sum, retroactive salary payment in 1929, and our family finances took a turn for the better. That fall, my father sent me to write examinations, and I was admitted to Belilios Public School for Girls. I savoured this precious opportunity to be educated.

The next year, I passed examinations for the Hong Kong Government Teachers' College and started night school as well. Because of the heavy pressure of studying night and day, I became ill after a year's hard work and had to drop out of night school in order to concentrate on passing the Junior and Senior School Certificate examinations. So, my attainment of the Graduation Diploma and a little bit of knowledge was the result of much arduous struggle.

Father had a solid grounding in Chinese literature and he expected a lot from his children when it came to Chinese culture. I remember one summer when he invited a famous accomplished teacher, Ng Sing-Chee, to be our Chinese tutor. This Mr. Ng had been thrown into jail for fifteen years because he had objected to the country squires of the New Territories leasing out ancestral land to the British. When he regained his freedom, he renamed himself Sing-Chee (meaning slow in awareness) in order to remind himself that he had been too late in recognizing the signs of the times. I deeply respected this old tutor. He had a way of arousing my interest in Chinese culture. As earthly fathers know how to give good gifts to their children, how much more will our Father in heaven give the Holy Spirit to those who ask Him? (Luke 11:13). Father loved his children and gave them knowledge of Chinese culture. This is yet another example of his love.

I graduated from secondary school in January of 1934 and was recruited as the superintendent of Li Shing Primary School in Ap Lee Chau, Aberdeen. The honorary headmaster was Mr. Li Tse-Ming, father of Canon Li Shiu-Keung. Mr. Li had established this charity school in commemoration of his father Mr. Li Shing in order to create educational opportunities for the children of fishermen. The post of superintendent had been vacant for a long time, as the children were poor, dirty, and mischievous. In addition, the school was hard to get to. Father was a good friend of Mr. Li Tse-Ming, and after talking it over, they arranged for me to fill this post. I happily abided by my father's decision, and therefore never tasted the bitter pill of "graduation means unemployment." So every morning, from far-away Shaukiwan, I trekked over land and sea to render my service with all my heart and mind.

I had always wanted to serve where no one else would go. My models were enterprising pioneers to backward places. Besides, in the Epistle to the Corinthians, St Paul says, "For you know the grace of our Lord Jesus Christ, that though he was rich, yet for your sakes he became poor, so that you through his poverty might become rich" (2 Cor. 8:9). I resolved to follow Christ's example—to work for the fortune of others and forget myself. I worked there for nine months, and the parents and the Education Department were very satisfied with the progress of my students. We need proper guidance to progress on our journey in life. "Train a child in the way he should go, and when he is old he will not turn from it" (Prov. 22:6). I treasured those innocent and charming, poor little children.

## 4. The Process of My Calling

In 1931, Bishop Duppuy of the Diocese of Chunghua Shungkunghui (Anglican Church of Victoria, Hong Kong and South China) ordained a British lady, Lucy Vincent, as deaconess at the St John's Cathedral in Hong Kong. Since I liked to be involved in new events in the church, I attended the solemn service with a fervent heart. I sat in the front pew and listened intently to Archdeacon Mok Sau-Tsang's sermon. (He later became suffragan bishop.) He proclaimed loudly, "Today, there is a British lady who is willing to proffer herself to the sacred office of deaconess in order to serve the Chinese Church. Is there a Chinese lady in the congregation to follow in her footsteps and commit herself to the Chinese Church?" I felt the challenge of this question deeply. I knelt down reverently and responded to God, "I am here. Please send me." However, I also asked, "Am I suitable?" All at once, I shared in what Isaiah had experienced in the temple. From then on, God's calling often reverberated in my ears.

In the autumn of 1934, I accepted a friend's invitation to spend a vacation in Guangzhou and visit Union Theological College. The principal was Dr. John Kunkle, an American. We took to each other immediately, and he invited me to become a seminary student. He had learned of my background through my friend and encouraged me to join the college as soon as possible. I told him that it would be hard for me to relinquish my teaching responsibilities and declined his kind invitation. When I was back in Hong Kong, I consulted the Rev. Tso See-Fong, rector of St Paul's Church. Through his ardent advocacy and the solid support of all the advisory board members, I reluctantly left the lovely children of Ap Lee Chau to study theology.

I had never dreamed of studying theology to become a priest. At the time, I had never even heard of women priests in the Anglican Church. I was seeking biblical knowledge only in order to serve the church in the areas that needed attention and to become a lay volunteer, useful to God.

Father had wished that one of his five sons would become a priest and serve the church. Unfortunately, none of them had an interest in the priesthood. As for me, I had been influenced by Christian thought from a very early age because of my family background. I remember my father teaching me to say the Lord's Prayer every night at bedtime when I was five or six years old: "Our Father, who art in Heaven, hallowed be Thy name..."

In 1918, my seven-year-old brother Yan-Yiu died after suffering convulsions from high fever. My parents were broken-hearted. A Mr. Sung Kui-Yan, a shepherd who was an ardent volunteer in spreading the gospel, frequently came to our house to console my parents with God's word. He said, "A little child is innocent. He went home to heaven to be among the angels and in God's bosom to enjoy eternal life." Because of this misfortune, my tender heart began to realize the religious truth of eternal life and eternal blessing in the kingdom of heaven.

After this painful event, my father had a better understanding of religious faith. He welcomed preachers' visits more avidly. Our living and dining rooms became Bible study classrooms and preaching halls for teachers and pastors. Mr. Wong Sut-Fong, pastor of Chinese Christian Church Yuen Long Church (father of Wong Yuk-Mui, General Secretary of the YWCA of Hong Kong), the Rev. Shing, and the Rev. Pei of the Church Missionary Society were all devoted friends of my father and frequent guests at our house. From the edification of such a Christian educational environment, I gradually developed an adoration for Christian faith.

Tam Sam-Koo of Hsinshing County, who had unfettered her bandaged feet, was a frequent visitor and Bible study leader. Another frequent visitor was Law Sau-Wan of Poklaw Village in Guangdong. They were both widowed. And although they were both semi-literate, they knew the Bible very well and were eager evangelists. They delivered the gospel to our door and thus deeply affected us, especially my mother.

I have reflected many times that truly I was born into a blessed family. I appreciated "How beautiful are the feet of those who bring good news!" (Rom. 10:15). These two ladies sowed the seeds of evangelism in my adolescence. Jesus said, "You did not choose me, but I chose you and appointed you to go and bear fruit" (John 15:16). Has not this adage come true? God's plan is thorough and workable.

## 5. Theological Training

I began my theological training at Union Theological College of Guangzhou in 1934. The "Union" of the Guangzhou Union Theological Seminary was due to the united sponsorship of the Church of Christ in China, the Methodist Church, and the Anglican Church.

The college was situated on the hilltop of White Crane Cave. The buildings looked over the sea and faced the busy marine traffic of White Swan Pond. In the shadow of a green forest was Fu Lee Tun Hall, the seminary. The campus was expansive, with large lecture halls. Small Western-style buildings that emerged from the shrubs in the meadow served as residences for the professors. Small gardens dotted the premise. Its neighbour was True Light Girls' School, famous for being scenic and known as "Home Sweet Home!" I spent two peaceful years in this fairyland, studying and meditating. I never anticipated the precipitous calamity that shattered our tranquillity.

### *The Tragedy of War*

In 1937, the July 7 Incident occurred. Japanese Imperialists attacked China. Battles broke out at Lo Kau Bridge near Beijing. Bombardment was everywhere. The Second World War had begun. The situation in North China became more tense by the day, and the raging war affected Guangzhou.

Guangzhou Christian leaders and the YMCA and YWCA adopted emergency measures to meet the needs of the time and formed a Christian first aid brigade. The seminary responded to the call and mobilized its students. I had been elected chairman of the Union Theological College Student Union, and I took on the responsibility of fund-raising. The first aid brigade needed helmets and uniform. Our New Testament professor, the Rev. Geoffrey Allen, who had recently arrived, donated generously. Thanks to the support of those who loved China, both residents and non-residents, the task of equipping the brigade was completed smoothly. I also took time out from fund-raising to attend the city-sponsored International Red Cross first aid training for ladies. Here I learned basic first aid techniques. The city government also assigned military officers to train all students and staff in marching, quick response, rapid movement, obeying commands, and the ins and outs of dug-outs. Being armed, we were truly Christian soldiers.

One day, Japanese bombers carried out carpet bombings of our area. When they had left, we were ordered to go to Shiguan Whang-sha Area to work. Everywhere I looked there was destruction. Fires were blazing all over the place. I discovered a trembling hand jutting out the side of a crumbled apartment building, underneath the giant cement and steel floor, and heard soft groans and cries for help. We tried to lift the cement block to free the trapped young girl, but no matter how hard we tried, we could not budge it. We had to jettison the rescue effort. I felt really helpless.

I turned and started searching other rooms for more victims. To my horror, I saw a woman seated in a rattan chair. Her upper body was covered by a burlap bag, and her tiny feet, having been traditionally bound, had kept her immobile and unable to escape from danger. My shoes were stuck to the floor in a pool of blood three inches deep. I moved onward into a yard and gaped at bloodied intestines hanging on the fence. The young man's body was lying at the side of the road. These were vivid examples of the extreme atrocities of fascism. Abject misery could be seen everywhere. The Old Testament prophet Micah's urgent call for world peace has been the common wish of all mankind all through history: "They will beat their swords into ploughshares and their spears into pruning hooks. Nation will not take up sword against nation, nor will they train for war anymore. Every man will sit under his own vine and under his own fig tree, and no one will make them afraid, for the Lord Almighty has spoken" (Mic. 4:3,4).

From July of 1937 to May of 1938, the Japanese Imperialist's foray into Guangzhou seemed imminent. Our final examinations at Union Theological College were held in May of 1938. Thus, we had to concentrate on preparing for exams through sirens and bombings. Our Mother country was threatened by enemies, and that incited us even more to improve our abilities and serve our people according to our duties. Patriotism welled up inside of me and jolted my heart in waves.

On the eve of June 1, 1938, I lined up with throngs of others to purchase a boat ticket at the quay of the Canton-Hong Kong ferry. I spread newspaper on the ground to rest upon so that I could set off for

Hong Kong in the morning. Among the passengers were some of my classmates and Mr. Li Shiu-Keung. He was responsible for the Department of Religion at Lingnam University then. Our conversation ranged from the political climate to religion, and he inspired me tremendously. Truly, to "hear his speech was better than studying for ten years."

Having just left the war-torn shambles of Guangzhou, life in Hong Kong across the water seemed peaceful and happy. The contrast between war and peace was beyond description. My ardent prayer was that God would grant peace. The bright hope of the prophet Isaiah surged into my mind: "For to us a child is born, to us a son is given. The government shall be upon his shoulders. And his name shall be called 'wonderful, counsellor, the mighty God, the everlasting Father, the Prince of Peace.'" The prophet painted us a future of endless glory. I sincerely hoped that this beautiful peace could be realized soon, to rescue the people from deep water and liberate them from helpless bondage. May God heed our prayers! A Chinese proverb goes, "Rather be a dog in peace, than be people in war." How appropriate!

## 6. Field Placement at All Saints' Church, Kowloon

The writer of Ecclesiastes (3:1,11,12) says, "There is a time for everything, and a season for every activity under heaven.... He has made everything beautiful in its time. He has also set eternity in the hearts of men; yet they cannot fathom what God has done from beginning to end. I know that there is nothing better for men than to be happy and do good while they live." The psalmist said it well: "The length of our days is seventy years—or eighty, if we have strength; yet their span is but trouble and sorrow, for they quickly pass, and we fly away" (Psa. 90:10).

I have always felt that God had His wonderful plan for each of His children. God chose His children in order to show His splendid will. Jesus, "having loved his own who were in the world ... now showed them the full extent of his love" (John 13:1). Moses blessed the Israelites and pronounced, "Your strength will equal your days" (Deut. 33:25).

After I received my diploma from the seminary in 1938, the diocese sent me to All Saints' Church of Kowloon, Hong Kong, to apprentice under the experienced Rev. Tsang Kai-Ngog (later archdeacon) for two years. The stalwart members of the Ladies Serving Group, such as Hung Ng-Koo, Mrs. Tat Choi-Fei, Mrs. Tsang Kai-Ngog, Mrs. Wong Wah-

Lam, Mrs. Yeung Yuk-Shu, Mrs. Chung Yu-Seng, Mrs. Wong Shum-Kan, and so on, along with advisory board members Mr. Robert Der, Mr. Tsang Koon-Kuk, Mr. Leung Kup-Man, Mr. Wong Ying-Yiu, and others, decorated the church premises for its fortieth anniversary celebration. They held a well-attended bazaar. The energetic youth broke new ground in forming a "Morning Star Club." This youth group was led by the Tsang Company (children of the Rev. Tsang). For the 1939 Christmas celebration, they presented a varied and colourful program. The congregation who attended packed the church hall.

I had been assigned two rooms as living quarters. There was a refugee, Mrs. Lau Han Mei-Ying from North China, who needed a place for her mother, a lay Anglican worker from Beijing, to stay temporarily. So I gave up one of my rooms for this lady. Later on, her son, Mr. Lau Chi-Ying, found her a flat on Nathan Road and she moved out. Soon after, two young women who were returning to China from Singapore found Guangzhou already lost to the Japanese. So they came to Kowloon, Hong Kong, and asked to stay with me a while, and I let them have the room. To follow Christ's teaching, "Whatever you did for one of the least of these brothers of mine, you did for me" (Matt. 25:40), to be able to solve the problems of the needy, is to feel a deep joy that no one can take away. The story of the Good Samaritan encourages us to be mindful of and helpful to those in need. Part of the work of All Saints' was to serve refugees, and I obeyed the Lord's teaching to help other people.

## 7. Transfer to Macau

I was transferred to Macau in the summer of 1940 to fill the young Rev. Peter Mak's post. The Rev. Mak had started an Anglican church here to minister to the Anglican refugees who fled to Macau from the fallen areas from Guangzhou Shekki to Giangmun.

At the time of my transfer, sinful practices were rampant in Macau. Gambling, debauchery, drugs, and prostitution were everywhere. As there was no appropriate male colleague available, I was transferred from All Saints', Kowloon. For two years, the Rev. Tsang Kei-Ngok had whole-heartedly trained me to be his assistant, and before my transfer to Macau, he tried unsuccessfully to persuade Bishop Hall to let me stay. "To obey is better than sacrifice, and to heed is better than the fat of rams" (1 Sam. 15:22). If this was intended for me, it did not matter whether I worked in the city or in the country. As long as I was needed, I would boldly go forward to accept the challenge.

Portuguese Macau was a night's journey by boat from Hong Kong. The Portuguese had colonized Macau four hundred years before. It had never been involved in any international wars, but had always remained neutral. Porto do Cerco was the crossover point along the Chinese-Portuguese border. China and Portugal always had friendly relations. Ever since China and Japan had gone to war, more and more people from inland China sought refuge in Macau.

The Macau Anglican Church was adjacent to Pigeon Nest Park. That was the cemetery of the first Christian missionary to China, the Rev. Morrison. The church rented the memorial chapel of the Rev. Morrison as the parish church, and these premises were under the managment of the British consulate.

In the summer of 1940, Bishop Hall sent Miss E. Atkins, principal of St Stephen's Girls' School in Hong Kong, to accompany me to Macau. As soon as we arrived, she arranged for me to visit the British consul and important Portuguese officials. She also arranged for me to stay at the Guangzhou YWCA hostel in Macau. Thus I built my first relationships within the social circles of Macau.

The previous rector, the Rev. Peter Mak, had been appointed by Bishop Ronald Hall to the Chinese Church of New Zealand. Sadly though, he was soon found to have brain cancer and was called home to heaven. He was a good shepherd and parishioners in Macau respected him very much and could not forget him.

## *My Work*

Coping assiduously with the endless influx of refugees entailed arranging for temporary room and board, sending the sick to hospital, providing for the interment of the dead. Luckily, parishioners were helpful and loving and co-operative. Everyone pitched in, so even the most difficult problems were easily solved.

At that time, Christian schools were moving from Guangzhou to Macau. These included Pui Ching, Pui To, Pui Ying, Lingnam Guangzhou Campus, and Union Girls' School. As well as serving the refugee parishioners, I looked after the needs of the students of these schools. I also accepted an invitation to help with Christian activities as a volunteer at Union Girls' School. I was responsible for evangelical and harvest services for three successive years. Every year, many decided to follow Christ and be baptized. In the last year, 1944, seventy-two young ladies were baptized.

The parish had always had a choir. Enthusiastic members, such as Mr. and Mrs. Ng Shun-Shin, Miss Cheung Shui-King, Mr. and Mrs. Wong Oi-Nam, Mr. Wong Oi-Sheng, Miss Chan Yau-King, Mr. Lau Hak-Ming, and many other young students who loved sacred music, participated. They offered their praises in Sunday worship, adding a solemnness to the liturgy and enhancing the worship atmosphere.

David Ho, whose father had lived in South Africa but had finally returned to China, was the crucifer of the parish who led the choir procession. When the war was over, he went back to South Africa. I was delighted to know that he had become a priest. I heard the good news when I met his sister in England, and was very happy.

Around 1940, the refugee centre of Shekki Anglican Church, operated by the Rev. Wong Fook-Ping, moved close to Macau. A camp was set up in the countryside of Yinkang. There were seventy or eighty refugee children and over twenty adults. Miss Liu Fung-Ching headed up the work inside the camp. Bishop Ronald Hall gave material and moral support. Every Thursday evening, a worker from the camp would come by boat to take me to the camp to lead baptism classes for both children and adults. I would stay at the camp overnight and officiate Morning Prayer the next morning. On Sunday, the class members came to our church to worship.

On May 22, 1941, I was ordered by Bishop Hall to come back to Hong Kong to be ordained as a deaconess, after which I returned to Macau. On Christmas Eve of the same year, Hong Kong fell to Japanese rule. During 1942 and 1943, more and more refugees fled Hong Kong for Macau. Our Anglican church had only about fifty seats, so folding chairs were set up inside and long benches were placed outside the front door of the building. Sunday worship was crowded, with a congregation of close to a hundred.

When I had first started there in 1940, there had been an English service every morning, led by the Rev. Thomas Broadfoot. He was a Canadian who had fled from Giangmun to Macau. A few weeks before Hong Kong fell, he flew back to Canada, and the British consul handed the responsibility for the English service to me. Recent refugees from

Hong Kong consisted of English-speaking Caucasians or Eurasians. From then on, the number of parishioners of international background who attended the morning service increased day by day.

The famous Hong Kong ophthalmologist Dr. Wong Shek-To said to me, "Our parish has few seats but hordes of people. The atmosphere is enthusiastic and worship is pious. In comparison, some Anglican parishes in Britain have huge churches, but those who attend services are few and far between. The atmosphere is cold and the church exists in form only." Jesus said, "The true worshippers will worship the Father in spirit and truth, for they are the kind of worshippers the Father seeks. God is spirit, and his worshippers must worship in spirit and in truth" (John 4:24). We used simple Anglican liturgy to worship and an intellectual approach in teaching.

Active members in the parish were plentiful, and included Dr. and Mrs. Luk Keng-Fei, Miss Ho Kam-Sim, Mr. and Mrs. Ng Shun-Shin, Miss Cheung Shui-King, Mrs. Tat Choi-Fei, Mr. and Mrs. Sung Shiu-Chuen, Dr. Cheng Pun-Hing, Dr. Cheng Cho-Man, Mr. Chan Pak-Chung (later ordained priest) and his wife, Mr. Leung Chiu-Chung, Miss Anderson, Miss Fok Kam-Ho, and Miss Fok Kam-Luen. There are many other unnamed heroes who were strong driving forces of church development.

## *The Plight of the People*

As the war raged on, the lives of ordinary citizens became more difficult. Greedy merchants controlled the price of rice. It was almost impossible to buy rice on the open market except for the set-price outlet, Chopsticks Base, which was far away and heavily queued. Otherwise, families with means had to rely on dependable leads to buy rice from the black market at four hundred Hong Kong dollars or Portugese currency for 100 catties (about 135 pounds).

The food shortage was so severe that "rice as pearls and fuel as jade" aptly describes the situation. After every cold spell or night of rain, the hunger-stricken fell into the gutters. Corpses lay everywhere. On my way to work, I would run into the passing "black carts" that picked up the dead bodies. The corpses were tightly packed like sardines in a tin, and the stench rose high in the sky. These were evidence of the sin of "man eating man." Yet Christ died for us when we were still sinners, and God's love for us is thus shown. Christ would feign to sacrifice and bleed on the cross, so our sins could be washed white as snow. To spread the gospel of redemption and call people to confess and repent are virtuous works we cannot decline.

Many of our parishioners became ill, and many died. Once, my sister in Christ Mrs. Leung was scared to go into the morgue to identify her husband after he died and asked me to do this for her. Following Christ's teaching to revere God and to love our fellow man, I gathered up enough courage to walk straight into the morgue of Keng-Wu Hospital. I looked over the countless rows of corpses lying on wooden planks and found one whose toes held a slip of paper with Mr. Leung's name on it. Although I was glad to identify the corpse, there was no coffin for burial. Fortunately, the undertaker was sympathetic and let me pledge my name for a coffin. The funeral was held and the family of Mr. Leung was thankful for God's mercy.

Mr. Lam Chung-Sang helped the Diocese of Hong Kong and Macau, serving as a liaison in administrative matters. His wife had contracted a serious lung disease, but she was not willing to go into the hospital. (Even if she had been willing, it was difficult to get admitted into a hospital.) Mrs. Chung-Sang's friends and family took care of her and arranged a make-shift canvas bed for her in an old shipyard near a beach. She wanted me to keep her company one day, to hold her hand in prayer and comfort her with gospel hymns. All the while I was with her, she vomited blood. The next day, she rested in peace. Her death bed brought her cease from her toils, yet the results of her work have followed her in the good fortune of her son.

## *Blessed with Provisions*

While I was under intense pressure to find rice to purchase, a very loving parishioner told me a piece of good news. The Portuguese government had perceived the widespread hunger from a report and undertook emergency measures. The government flung open its doors to let citizens register to buy rice. Without hesitation, I ran to the Portuguese Governor's office. At the side of the stairs to the office were fully armed soldiers. From wit born under pressure, I spoke to them in English and convinced them to let me go straight to the office. God was with me, and my application to purchase five huge burlap bags of rice at the fair price, each weighing two hundred pounds, was approved. Nevertheless, we had to wait patiently at the quay each day for the rice to be shipped from Hong Kong.

Luckily, some active parishioners took turns waiting, and after a month's delay, we received a thousand pounds of rice. As a result, parishioners who were close to starving received temporary relief and were therefore more staunch in their belief that God takes care of His children. Jesus said, "Man does not live on bread alone, but on every word that comes from the mouth of God." We could be more relaxed now, with provisions, but spiritual nurturing needed to increase.

### *The Problem of Celebrating Eucharist*

Our parish held a Communion service once a month. Either the Rev. Wong Fook-Ping came from Shekki to celebrate the service or the Rev. Tsang Kei-Ngok from Hong Kong took it on. However, since Hong Kong had fallen, the priests dared not risk their lives crossing the Japanese war front in order to celebrate Communion. Yet, with the world in turmoil and lives unsettled, the faithful thirsted for the Lord's body and blood to give solace and strength in their arduous days.

I had been ordained as deaconess in May of 1941 and could not act out a priest's prerogative to satisfy the needs of parishioners. In order to deal with the special circumstance, the Rev. Wong Fook-Ping suggested to Bishop Mok Sau-Tsang that he grant special permission for me to celebrate Holy Communion. On Easter Day of 1942, I obeyed Bishop Mok's order to start celebrating Eucharist.

## 8. Grateful and Unforgettable

When Hong Kong had fallen into Japanese hands, the Guangzhou YWCA, which was in Macau, had closed its hostel for lack of financial support. This left only a well-weathered executive secretary, Ms. Chan Shuet-Tung, in the city office to maintain communication with its members. Since I was a board member of the YWCA, Ms. Chan Shuet-Tang and I took care to uphold various worthwhile activities for the ladies. At that time, my stipend from the Hong Kong Diocese had ceased to arrive. After Hong Kong had fallen, the diocese had tried to send me two hundred dollars through a parishioner who was fleeing to Macau. Unfortunately, this refugee used the money to make ends meet.

Seeing my plight, the principal of Union Girls' Secondary School, Liu Fung-Ling, arranged room and board for me at her school. Later, Bishop Mok Shau-Tsang came to Macau. After conferring with the advisory board members, he took care of my living expenses and paid what I owed the school for my room and board. It was not until my father came to Macau that my livelihood was secured. Isn't it clear that God takes utmost care of His children, as much as our hairs have been counted? During this period, Principal Liu took loving care of me. Her graciousness was truly unforgettable.

## 9. Braving Danger to Save My Father

One day in 1942, a Hong Kong Christian refugee to Macau sent me a note from a relative of mine. The note urged me to send for my ill and destitute father who was still in Yuen Long, Hong Kong. Luckily, with the assistance of a helpful and trustworthy Christian, Mr. Lam Chung-Sang, I was able to personally run the Japanese blockade to bring my father to Macau.

My experiences with the British consul also helped. Some of the parishioners who fled to Macau were getting monthly Subsidies for Widows from the British consulate, while others were retired civil servants. Fortunately, the British consul had such confidence in me that those Anglican parishioners who qualified for any living subsidies, pension, or travel allowances to Chungking or Chujiang needed only my signature as witness in order to receive financial support. I therefore boldly formulated a plan to save my father from his deep water and presented it to him. He promised to pay my father's pension as a retired British schoolmaster plus all the payments missed since Hong Kong had fallen if father arrived safely. The consul even lent me ten Hong Kong dollars for the fare I needed to smuggle into Hong Kong.

I sewed the ten dollars into my collar and disguised myself as a maid. Under the leadership of Mr. Lam Chung-Sang, a group of us tried to sail out to sea in a fishing boat. Three times we attempted to set off in stormy weather from Macau to the New Territories in Hong Kong, the last time at dusk. When the fishing boat was breaking waves in full sail, we spotted a pirate ship charging towards us. The fisherman ordered all of us to throw the fishnet overboard and pretend we were trying to pull the net in. All the passengers co-operated. Knowing that I was a missionary, they jointly urged me to get below deck to pray. I gladly obeyed and knelt down in sincere intercession, imploring God to show His mercy, forgive our sins known and unknown, and grant us peace that passes understanding. Thinking that we were merely poor fishermen with no profitable booty, the bandits turned and sailed away.

As the night deepened, the sea became very dim. We were rowing towards our destination—Tuen Mun of the New Territories. Suddenly a motorboat puttered into hearing range. It was a Japanese patrol boat on its rounds and our situation became very dangerous. Many passengers threw themselves into the sea and tried to swim towards the shore of a nearby bay. Even though I could hardly swim, I prepared to jump into the water. Then, at the most critical moment, rain suddenly began to pour down. Dark clouds impaired the vision of those in the Japanese patrol boat as we expeditiously withdrew into the closest bay.

When the rain stopped, we hurried to Tuen Mun Bay where many boats were gathered. I hopped from boat to boat and then ran to ask for help from the church in Tuen Mun. It was around three or four in the morning when I banged on the church door, and a youth came to answer. I identified myself, and he immediately took me to my parent's home on his bicycle. My parents opened the back door for me to slip in. Soon after, my father and I drove straight to Kowloon in a farm merchant's lorry to stay over at a relative's. (At the time, my brother Hon-Yiu was employed by this produce merchant, so we could use the lorry.) We quickly performed the necessary procedures for our exit and boarded the Japanese ferry bound for Macau, with Bishop Mok Shau-Tsang in our company.

We stopped over in Hong Kong. Father, my third sister Kwai-Cheung, and I were shopping at Central District in Hong Kong when we met two passengers who had been on the same boat as I. They proclaimed enthusiastically, "Miss Li, your God is the true God, and He listened to you!" They told me that two other fishing boats had set off from Macau at about the same time as ours. All the persons on board the other two boats were slaughtered by Japanese guards, staining the sea red. This experience paralleled Moses' leading of the Israelites across the Red Sea. God separated the water so the Israelites could pass in safety. Then, the Ten Commandments stated that one must "honour your parents so you may live long." This maxim transcends all cultures. An old Chinese adage goes, "A tree wished to be still, but the wind would not rest. A son wished to be pious, but the parents had rested." As children, it is never too soon to practice piety in order to repay the gracious labours of our parents.

## 10. Ordination to Priesthood

In late December of 1943, I received a letter from Bishop Ronald Hall from Chungking inviting me to the Anglican Church of Shaoqing, Guangdong, to be ordained as priest. This was to take place on January 25, 1944 (the Feast of the Conversion of St Paul). In the winter of 1943, Bishop Hall had taken a vacation in England and returned to Chungking. Upon his return, he heard of my work through some church members from Macau. He was very excited and thought that I should be ordained a priest. In his opinion, God's work would reap better results if I had the proper title.

### *Journey to the Ordination Ceremony*

Because of the ardent support of advisory board members and parishioners, I decided to proceed to my destination, Hsinxing, as per the invitation to the Rev. Lai Kei-Chong's Chung Hua Sheng Kung Hui Parish where I would meet Bishop Hall.

Travelling during war time was quite an arduous feat from the point of view of safety. From Macau, I took a ferry to Guangzhou, transferred by boat to Giangmun, and from Giangmun, cycled to a village at the foot of a big mountain. There I stayed overnight at a Christian household suggested by a friend of mine. Through the assistance of a Giangmun parishioner, Mr. Chiu Ping-Foo, a sedan-chair was hired. In the first light of dawn, we rounded the bend of the mountain and journeyed on through the meandering mazes of footpaths. We pressed onward till sundown, when a light mist descended. We then asked for lodging at a police station in the mountain. After I showed him Bishop Hall's letter, the police chief let me stay in a guards' room.

Even though the place was filthy, I slept very soundly, thinking that God would protect me for doing His work and that the angels would look after me. The next morning, the police chief ordered six armed police, three in front and three at the back, to guard me through my journey. When we passed a town, the townspeople all murmured that this lady must be from the family of an important governor! In fact, God loves those who belong to Him to the utmost. The guards only said goodbye to me when we had left the rogue-infested area.

The two sedan-chair carriers comforted me again and again: "Relax, lady. We are honest peasants. Though we are passing through isolated terrain and poor areas, we will protect you." By trusting in their loyalty and honesty, I was able to freely enjoy the natural beauty of the land that God created. Finally, we reached a plain, and through an expansive and vibrant emerald bamboo forest lay Hsinxing Anglican Church. Here, I got off the sedan-chair to meet Bishop Hall.

With God's protection, Bishop Hall, the Rev. Lai, and myself all arrived safely and promptly. As we met, we all knelt down immediately to offer our prayer of thanksgiving. The three of us prayed and meditated for two days before we set off to Shaoqing by ferry, via a tributary of Shigiang. We passed by the villages Yuenfou and Yaukoo and picked up Mr. Pang Yan-Cheung (later ordained priest, and rector of the Church of the Good Shepherd in Vancouver) to attend my ordination ceremony.

## The Ceremony

The Rev. Lai Kei-Chong was rector of both Hsinxing and Shaoqing parishes. He successfully rallied many Christian brothers and sisters from both areas to attend the ordination service, which was presided over by Bishop Hall himself. Bishop Hall used the liturgy for Ordination of Priests according to the Anglican canon and posed questions to examine my faith. To every question he asked, I would immediately volunteer, with sincere reverence, "I will."

Among those who joined in thanksgiving were the family of Mr. Chiu Pei-Tak, who had just arrived from Hsinhui, leaders of the local Chinese Holiness Church and its congregation, plus forty or so ladies from the Ming-Sum Hospital (for the Blind).

On that afternoon, Bishop Hall held a press conference, for which I was the interpreter. The journalists were primarily interested in politics and could not have cared less about the topic of religion. After the official business was over, I took advantage of the opportunity to visit towns behind the battle lines, such as Chujiang and Guilin. Then I boarded a train bound for Wujou where I was to set sail to Macau via Guangzhou.

At that time, an old classmate of mine, Dr. Wang Hang-Ching, was working at SeeTat Hospital in Wujou. During my visit with her, she put me up at the hospital, and I preached there for two days. This unexpected opportunity to spread the gospel right after my ordination brought me great joy! St Paul was an ardent evangelist. His words encouraged me: "When I preach the gospel, I cannot boast, for I am compelled to preach. Woe to me if I do not preach the gospel!" (I Cor. 9:16).

Upon my safe return to Macau, my parishioners and members of the youth group threw a celebration and a dinner party for me, and gave me gifts to commemorate the occasion. Not long after, I was invited by the Union Girls School to preach for my third and last time at their Evangelistic Harvest event. As I preached, I could feel the Spirit bracing me even more than the two previous times. Having just received God's benedictions, I felt more abundant and much empowered with new strength. I wanted to sing, "New every morning is the love / Our wakening and uprising prove... / Restored to life and power and thought" (*Hymns of Universal Praise*, No. 381).

## 11. The Controversy over Ordaining Women

In the summer of 1945, peace was declared throughout the world. The fireworks set off to celebrate the tidings shook Macau. Soon, in 1946, I received a letter from Bishop Hall's secretary, the Rev. George She (also a lawyer), asking me to come to Hong Kong for a meeting. At the meeting, I was quickly told that Bishop Hall had broken church canon law to ordain me as a priest, and hence had been denounced and criticized by the Archbishop of Canterbury. Either Bishop Hall must resign as bishop or I must give up the title of priest.

When first told of this problem, I was quite perturbed. I gave serious thought as to whether I should step down or stay on. Through a moment of deep meditation in which I prayed for God's guidance, and the constant working of the Holy Spirit, I suddenly saw the light. I realized that I should see my personal prestige as worthless for I was merely a small servant of the Lord. As the psalmist put it, "I am a worm" (Psa. 22:6).

I voluntarily and whole-heartedly supported Bishop Hall in upholding his holy office as bishop. He was a man of deep spirituality. Not only was he influential in the Chinese Church, but his international contributions were also large. I was willing to give up my title of priest, but I knew that having been ordained, I had to follow the order throughout my life. I had to be obedient without minding small matters and, without remorse, serve the church with my best effort, free from secular care. This is my philosophy of life. No one can take away the peace that comes from completing one's responsibilities to history and fulfilling God's will. Jesus' teaching is very precious: "No one who puts his hand to the plow and looks back is fit for service in the kingdom of God" (Luke 9:62), and, "Any of you who does not give up everything he has cannot be my disciple" (Luke 14:33). Thence, I gladly pressed on in serving God and continued with my duties.

## 12. Establishing a Permanent Base in Macau

After peace was proclaimed throughout the world, and Japanese Imperialists had surrendered, the population in Macau dropped drastically. Immigrant parishioners moved back to their homelands in droves in order to rebuild their lives. One after another, Christian schools left their make-shift campuses to resume operating in Guangzhou. Sunday attendance at church gradually declined, and Bishop Hall informed me that I was being transferred to Lienzhou of Hepu in Guangdong Province.

Before my transfer from Macau, I pondered over the fact that the Chunghua Shungkunghui did not have its own church premise. As church members could enjoy peace and a new beginning after the war by the mercy of God, I decided to bravely suggest to each member that he or she offer a thanksgiving donation towards a permanent church building as the home of the Macau parish.

After earnest prayers, I first contacted a Mr. Cheung Yu-Chiu to discuss purchasing a church building. He was generous and evangelistic and immediately donated ten thousand Hong Kong dollars. This huge sum boosted my confidence and my faith, and for days I travelled around Guangzhou, Hong Kong, and Macau without rest, visiting parishioners to invite them to participate in this thanksgiving drive. Consequently, all pitched in. The church choir held a concert, with Miss Cheung Shui-King (Mrs. Ng Shun-Sin) singing a solo, and Mrs. Ma Siu-Leung and all choir members raised one thousand dollars towards the building fund.

Property prices in Macau had plummeted after the war. There was an old hotel on Pedro Nolasco da Silvia listed for sale at a low price. Even though we had not gathered enough donations, the Anglican Diocese of Victoria, Hong Kong, and South China made up for the difference. In January of 1947, I had to leave for my post in Hepu. On the eve of leaving Macau, I made sure that Bishop Mo Yung-Yin of Guangzhou would come to Macau to complete the building purchasing agreements. Faithful parishioners Dr. Luk Kang-Fei and Mr. Chan Pak-Chung took up the responsibilities of renovating the hotel into an Anglican church building.

Bishop Hall asked for my help in selecting a suitable candidate to maintain the work in Macau. I suggested that it would be best to ordain Mr. Chan Pak-Chung as honorary priest to take charge, as he had always been eager to serve the church and had the leisure to do so. The bishop adopted my suggestion, and the congregation received an apt pastor.

# Part Two
# *1947–1980*

✢ ✢ ✢

## 13. Reminiscences of Hepu

In January 1947, I set off for Hepu to take up my post as rector at St. Barnabas Church, together with Suffragan Bishop Halward, the Rev. Wittenbach, secretary of the Church Missionary Society Mrs. Tsang Kei-Ngok, a lady missionary of Beihai Wong Kum-Yan, and the aunt of parishioner Cheung King-Yan. We travelled by road from Guangzhou Bay through Suichi County towards Beihai, Hepu. As this was during China's civil war years, we encountered guerrilla activity along our way. Thanks to the governing Kuomintang, who were eager to protect foreign friends travelling in our party, armed guards were sent to escort us to safety through the troubled area. While on the waters, God was with us through the raging storm, and we arrived at our destination safe and sound.

St Barnabas Church of Hepu had been established in 1918 by three or four zealous British women of the Church Missionary Society. When the Sino-Japanese war had broken out, the British ladies had retreated to their homeland, and all religious activities ceased until peace was proclaimed. The church grounds were extensive, with sprawling lush green lawns, dense fruit groves, and blooming flowers. The people called it the "British Place." The spire-topped St Barnabas, a comfortable two-storey house called the Maiden's House (the rectory), a small hospital, and three other small buildings dotted the picturesque landscape.

When we reached Hepu, Bishop Halward introduced me to the parishioners as "Deaconess." It was not until the spring of 1949 when Bishop Hall visited the Shungkunghui of Hepu that he corrected the parishioners by emphasizing that I should be hailed "priest." Nevertheless, the communion bread and wine were consecrated by Archdeacon Tsang Kei-Ngok of Beihai and forwarded to me.

Soon after our arrival, I took on the work of restarting the church. For a short time, I visited former church members who lived in town. With the ardent support of members such as Mr. and Mrs. Chan Wing-Tung and family, who loved the Lord dearly, Sunday worship was reintroduced. At first, there were only thirty or so members, but gradually, through evangelism, the number of Sunday worshippers increased. Bishop Hall encouraged us to make full use of all of the church properties before the Liberation, when the Kuomintang government would be toppled by the Communists. By so doing, the church might be able to retain these properties and also demonstrate the proper attitude for the church of serving society. Jesus taught us that "the Son of Man had not come to be served but to serve."

We tried our best to open an advanced nursery to commemorate Bishop Mok Shau-Tsang and to start a small primary school. Female evangelist Tam Shau-Yuen devoted much of her energy to supporting the education and nursery work. There was a terrible tradition of despising female babies in Hepu. In response, we established a Po-Yan (Altruist) Maternity Branch Hospital so that, for a reasonable fee, pregnant women could stay in a peaceful environment and receive proper health care. Moreover, we could take the opportunity to educate the women to treasure their baby girls. We told them that Jesus loves babies of both sexes, and boys and girls should be given the same level of education. When the girls matured, they could contribute to society as much as the boys.

The work of this obstetrics hospital was greatly supported by the female doctor Lam Yan and midwife Li Kwai-Cheung, my sister. Their help was much appreciated.

## *Friends of Christ Society*

Guangshi Hepu is also named Lienzhou. Provincial Lienzhou Secondary School was the most eminent of the three secondary schools in Hepu and a cultural centre of southwestern Guangdong. It nurtured numerous brilliant students to serve the country and society. I was hired by the school as an English teacher for a few terms and developed deep friendships with my colleagues and students. They gave me a lot of encouragement. I can recall vividly the day in 1948 when I was sent by the diocese as a delegate to visit the United States of America. The students at Lienzhou Secondary formed a marching band from the school to the bus terminal to give me a spirited send-off. The majestic music attracted quite a horde from every laneway to say farewell.

For youth catechism, I formed both a Chinese and an English Bible study class. I used Bishop Hall's "Life of Jesus" as a study guide, which was excellent for beginners. We also followed St Luke's Church of Beihai in organizing a Friends of Christ Society so that the young people could learn to love the church through fellowship life.

St Andrew, who was eager to lead others to Christ, was the model of our Society. Young people were called to win friends for Christ. The Society had its own rules and regulations, and members were given badges. A solemn candlelight ceremony marked the induction of each member into the Society.

The church became a popular activity centre for the young people after school. Some followed Christian friends and joined the choir, attended Sunday worship, and helped to landscape the garden and beautify the church. Their spiritual life grew rapidly in such a pleasant environment. There were also sports activities and the young people published two magazines, *The Living Fountain* and *Everflowing*. These pieces of literature helped to report all church activities, link up other Christians outside of the county, and serve as reports to the diocese.

## *Forming the Three-Self Movement*

After China was liberated in 1949, a Mr. Wu Yiao-Chung and some avant-garde Christians met with Premier Chou En-Lai to discuss the direction that Chinese churches should follow in New China. After intensive deliberation, the way of "self-rule, self-supporting and self-propagation"—the Three-Self Movement—was deemed the proper Christian and patriotic way to go.

In 1950, I voluntarily initiated a joint study for the three denominations in Hepu, the Lutherans, the Seventh Day Adventists, and the Anglicans, to learn about the content, meaning, and practicality of the Three-Self Movement.

Land reform was instituted in 1951, and after the Feast of Conversion of St Paul on January 25, the parish was closed down. Even though I was part of the driving force behind the Three-Self Movement, the reality of the new ways caused me inner turmoil. For the moment, I could not share the people's standpoint, and my soul searching was a burden to me spiritually. After diligent Bible studies and meditation, a passage from

Romans 13:1,2 finally shed light for me: "Everyone must submit himself to the governing authorities, for there is no authority except that which God has established. The authorities that exist have been established by God. Consequently, he who rebels against the authority is rebelling against what God has instituted, and those who do so will bring judgment on themselves." With the Holy Spirit working within me, I could stride forward in progress with the tide.

## 14. Further Studies in Beijing

The People's government took over the church buildings in stages, and the nursery, primary school, and maternity hospital were soon closed down. We were sent to live in the estate of a neighbouring esquire, Wong Chit-Man. The incumbent of the Seventh Day Adventist So King-Yat and his family were also living there. We each had a room and shared the kitchen.

At that time, the communique Tien Fung (Heavenly Wind) reported that Yenjing Seminary in Beijing was accepting working clergy members to study theology more suitable to New China. I therefore sent in my application for retraining and was soon accepted by the principal Dr. T. C. Chao and the admissions committee. I was scheduled to start classes in January of 1952. I was happy knowing I would soon be a student again, and I immediately reported to Archdeacon Kong Chi-Wing of Beihai in order to wrap up the work at Hepu. After everything was settled, it was still more than six months before I received a pass to travel to Beijing through Guangzhou.

It was cold and snowing when I reached Yenjing Union Theological College in January of 1952. The whole country was at the peak of an unprecedented, anti-Imperialist, patriotic movement. Scrutiny, criticism, classes, and self-criticism became part of my daily experience. Several factors led to my feeling oppressed: I had just arrived and was a total stranger to the area and the people, I was caught in the midst of a serious political climate, and I had a poor grasp of Mandarin.

The members of my discussion group were not understanding at all. "There are only two new students accepted from all over the country. How did you become one, into post-graduate studies, even?" they demanded. "You must be an Imperialist," they charged. "Bishop Hall broke tradition to ordain you as the first woman priest. He ordained Chao Tse-

Chen a deacon after transferring him to the Anglican Church from another denomination and, within the hour, ordained him a priest, which was also extraordinary." Based on these two events, they accused Dr. Chao and me of being Bishop Hall's spies, especially placed in Beijing amidst the first anti-Imperialist patriotic movement. Leaders of the political movements strongly suspected us of plotting to damage the new political powers under the direction of Bishop Hall.

Challenges and criticisms continued to storm down on me from the others in the discussion group and I responded with acquiescence. As I was naive about politics, no words of mine, neither oral nor written, could appease them. One day, a fanatic member of the group led me into a classroom to show me my political identity, scrawled on the blackboard in huge characters—"SPY." My agony was indescribable. Another day, a female group member ordered me to clean the toilets of the dormitory. I had to obey patiently. The teachers and students whom I met after meals or walking along corridors would not speak to me. They cast despising glances at me to express their animosity. While being ostracized so callously, I could not feel a hint anywhere in the seminary of the command to "love one another" as taught by Jesus.

Since I was unable to adjust my ideology quickly enough, I felt isolated and forlorn. Satan tried fiercely to pull me down to hell. Every night after supper, I strolled beside a lake on campus, appreciating the weeping willows and the songs of the slight yellow birds skipping from tree to tree. In comparison, I felt like a bird captured in a cage of political struggle, having lost its freedom, joy, and peace. During a moment of weakness, I thought of throwing myself into the lake and ending my miserable life. This pessimistic notion churned in my brain for a whole week.

One evening, as I was lost in frenzied thought, a stream of golden light shimmered towards me through the evening haze. At that moment, a small voice reminded me that our physical form comes from God, and houses a precious soul. Besides, as a Chinese proverb asserted, "We receive our skin and bodies from our parents and must not hurt or destroy them." How can we slight life? Can the soul be saved through suicide? Even the suicide of a lay person is a disgrace to God. How much more would the suicide of an ordained servant of God with a priestly office shame and despoil the church! Moreover, my political detractors would view my suicide as an admission of guilt. These revelations were like the gracious Light that shone on St Paul when he was on his way to Damascus. My soul immediately awoke, and I stood in silence. Holding onto Saviour Jesus, I prayed earnestly. Patiently and resolutely, I focused my attention on every single suspicion held against me. Without reserve, I accounted for them to God. I also prayed for the wisdom to fulfil my duties towards my people.

Through the mercy and blessings of God, I was pleasantly surprised one April afternoon when Vice-Principal Chiang Ye-Zen sought me out. He grabbed my arm and told me happily, "The people have understood you." I had been cleared of the accusation of being a spy. Instantly, a large weight was lifted from my shoulders, my spirit was revived, and I felt unsurpassed delight. I poured my heart out in an article entitled "From Darkness into Light," and in the blink of an eye, my classmates had posted it on the blackboard for all to see. I felt a wonderful joy and peace at finally winning the confidence and trust of the others.

My education in Beijing lasted three terms. Time quickly flew by. At last the nine courses ended, concluding with final examinations. My diligence and effort yielded success. St Paul comforted me with these words: "We know that all things work together for good to them that love God, those who have been called according to his purpose" (Rom. 8:28). What I had learned in Patriotism and Spirituality during my Beijing studies deeply affected me.

## 15. Back to Guangzhou
### Teaching at the Seminary

In the summer of 1953, I was appointed by Bishop Mo Yung to teach at my alma mater, Union Theological College of Guangzhou, and assist at the Anglican cathedral, The Church of Our Saviour. Just before the Liberation, the college had moved to the Hong-Lok (Recreation) Area to merge with Lingnam University. The new college was located at the south entrance of the university. A new and enlarged lecture hall had been built, and professors and students had received new dormitories.

During 1953 and 1954, I taught students there the necessity of adopting the way of the Three-Self Movement. Our goal was to clear the slanderous insult that "one more Christian means one less patriot" and the vilification of Christianity as a foreigners' religion. We had to build a holy church suitable to China's situation that would win the trust and respect of the people. I also taught Church History and the Central Basic Cultural Program, and served as the Dean of Women.

In the autumn of 1954, Chung Shan University moved into Lingnam University. Since Chung Shan expressed atheistic views contrary to the teachings of the college, it was only logical to go our separate ways. The theological college sold all of its buildings to Chung Shan for one hundred thousand renminbi (Chinese currency).

The college then moved to Fangchuen Area into two buildings rented from the Lutheran Church. Two years later, the Lutheran Church joined the union to expand the work of nurturing young people to develop the church, and the college moved again, this time to Tungshan Area where the Baptist Seminary had been. The new location was tranquil, although it was within a busy section. The gardens were beautiful. The air was filled with the chirps of birds and the fragrance of flowers. It was located on top of Tungshan (East Hill), and the scenery was very pleasant. Diligent students from all over the province came here to receive theological training.

In 1957, the college held a Holy Communion service to celebrate Christmas. Principal Kwong Ning-Fat invited me to celebrate according to the Anglican Eucharistic rite. All the staff and students of the college came to receive spiritual nourishment. Under shimmering candlelight, we had a solemn and restrained liturgy full of history and tradition to commemorate the birth of Jesus and receive God's grace with joy. I remembered what St Paul said: "Speaking the truth in love, we will in all things grow up into him who is the Head, that is, Christ. From him the whole body, joined and held together by every supporting ligament, grows and builds itself up in love, as each part does its work" (Eph. 4:15,16). This experience manifested the first stage of church unification.

## *Sent Down to the Farms*

In 1958, I was instructed by Principal Kwong to take all the seminary students to join with the teachers and pastors of the city and go to the communes to do labour. The teaching staff remaining in the college had to attend political study meetings, together with their fellow church workers in the city. When those teachers and pastors who were engaged in steel making had completed their assignment and launched a satellite into orbit, we teachers and students joined the company of all the other teachers and pastors to form a massive "Christian Army." We marched to the northern part of the Panyu County in Guangdong Province to open up virgin land and create a new farm there. Halfway up the hill in Jianggaozhan, our pioneering work consisted of rearing sheep, poultry, and rabbits, growing pineapples and vegetables, and digging a fish pond to raise fish. Some of the seminary students had been raised on farms, and they were energetic and diligent in their labour.

There were times of serious ideological struggle for me while working on the farm. As I had never had to do a great deal of physical labour, I was constantly worried about not having enough strength to complete my tasks. However, I thought of labour as sacred and obedient to God's will, and I willingly immersed myself in my training, hoping I could stand the test.

My assigned tasks on the farm were to rear poultry and keep rabbits on the side. At first, rearing poultry was relatively easy. After harvests, I let the chickens peck up the leftover grains. The chickens were well fed and fattened quickly, and I was duly praised. After the onset of winter, however, it became difficult to provide feed for the two to three hundred chickens. Every day I had to argue and bicker with the head of the farm for feed. In the end, the head suggested that I adopt the proletarian view and solve the problem myself. He advised me to dig a trench on the hill. In the trench I was to place pine branches from the trees, bury them, and irrigate them with the water used for cleaning rice. This would breed termites, which would supply the protein content of the chicken feed. In practise, however, this produced tiny yellow ants visible only through a magnifying glass.

The second piece of advice the farm head gave me was to plant grass seeds on the rolling hills and take the chickens to far-off hills to graze. I carried the first basketful of chickens there, and those smart chickens followed me home when I turned to get the second batch. Hence, I was nicknamed "Captain of the Chickens." Because of a lack of food, many of the chickens died. New chickens were brought in and introduced diseases that wrecked the entire farm. The appearance of a chicken plague prompted compulsory autopsies of the dead chickens, which fortunately proved that I had not murdered them. What a relief! Nevertheless, I could not escape criticism. I once complained, "A precious lady is sold as a slave girl; exquisite hardwood is used as firewood." That gave my colleagues even more ammunition with which to castigate me.

At night, all of us who were cleric comrades had to work under gaslight, digging out a fish pond and making bricks with the earth. When the bricks had dried, they were used in the construction of a new sleeping quarters on the hillside. When completed, the new quarters saved us the hour-long walk to the hills every morning. I was lucky to be assigned a bed in the new building. I did not have to get up early for the trek, and I was happy, never anticipating that this good fortune would almost cost me my life.

Late one night, I suddenly developed a high fever and felt very dizzy. My heartbeat was frighteningly rapid. All night long, I could not sleep. Though I was very tired in the morning, I forced myself to get up and prepare for work. As I was washing my face, I noticed some marks on my left wrist that looked like bites from a poisonous insect. In that remote place, there were no physicians or medicines available, and, moreover, I did not want to speak out for fear of being criticized for making a fuss. Innovation was called for, and I used my own saliva as an ointment to soothe my wounds. Later that day, during noon siesta, I found a black centipede as long as my finger while making my bed. Evidently it had pinched me, depositing its venom in my body. So, my colleagues all gathered to help catch the pest and burn it. At that moment, I thought of what Jesus said when sending out his disciples: "I have given you authority to trample on snakes and scorpions and to overcome all the power of the enemy; nothing will harm you" (Luke 10:19). God is love. His wonderful work protected my life, just as the psalmist said: "The Lord is my rock, my fortress and my deliverer, my God is my rock, in whom I take refuge. He is my shield and the horn of my salvation, my stronghold" (Psa. 18:2).

The students laboured in the communes for eighteen months, and I, for another half a year. The principal of the college understood that the political movement would deepen, and religion might no longer be tolerated. He therefore arranged for the students to be sent back to classes in order to graduate. In 1960, the seminary was closed.

## *Factory Labour*

After my months of labour on the farm, I was sent, in 1960, to work in the Three-Self Movement "Forward" factory. The Movement had started a factory using the Seven-Banyan Church of Christ in China. This factory produced products such as water pipes, baking powder, syringes, glued paper cartons, waxed candy wrappers, plastic films, and so on.

When I was first sent down to the factory, I worked at packaging syringes. Later, I was transferred to the paper cartons gluing department located in the nearby Six-Banyan Monastery and was responsible for moving the wet cartons into the yard so they could dry in the sun. After a hundred days of work there, I was transferred back to the original place to work at waxing candy wrappers. The wax cauldron had a temperature of three thousand degrees. Since there was no air-conditioning, workers there in the summer were severely punished by the heat. Everyday I had to bring seven or eight towels to work, to dry the sweat off my back and chest so I would not catch a cold.

One night, I was working the night shift. Pastor Lee Tak-Fai and a janitor were guarding the door while I was resting in the middle of the factory. Since the weather was very hot and my mosquito-net was worn out, swarms of mosquitoes prevented me from sleeping. At midnight, I realized that smoke was filling the factory. I got up immediately and saw that the huge wax cauldron was not closed properly. Thick and heavy clumps of melting wax were spilling from it. Immediately, I ran to the door to wake the two men, and we choked off the cauldron with wet coals. At last, we averted the danger of fire. The factory was filled with paper and other flammable objects. If a fire had broken out, the lives and property of all those living on the entire street would have gone up in smoke. Even though at that time efforts had increased to stamp out all theistic thoughts, my appreciation deepened that "the Lord is my strength and my song; he has become my salvation" (Psa. 118:14); "My help comes from the Lord, the Maker of heaven and earth" (Psa. 121:2). Atheism was never able to replace my staunch faith in God throughout my entire life. God is the true God who is always with me. God is worthy of adoration.

There was once a time when we were obliged every morning before work to pay respect to Chairman Mao in front of his portrait and recite passages from his Red Book. The same rite was repeated after work. I underwent countless atheistic urgings, but large and small daily experiences manifested the blessings of God, and feelings of thanksgiving naturally welled up within me. God's grace is boundless. It is true that God's grace is enough for us, and God's love and mercy are eternal.

## 16. A Facade of Peace and Prosperity

Between 1960 and the summer of 1966, one could say that our society appeared generally peaceful. The reason for this was the Great Leap

Forward, the development of communal programs and the national steel-making program. The work of the church diminished. All citizens concentrated their efforts on the various movements, and the activities of Sunday worship consequently declined. Due to the gathering of materials to make steel, all metallic objects in the churches, such as crosses, donation plates, stained glass windows, iron gates, and vessels for Holy Communion were confiscated by the government and thrown into the steel cauldron.

The YWCA was flourishing at that time. Membership was increasing. Active members were solicited to stage drama productions in order to satisfy the cultural needs of members and to entertain the leader comrades of the Provincial People's Business Promotion Committee. I was an active member then, and helped to stage short contemporary plays such as "One Family Under the White Cloud Hill" and "Spring Fantasy in Taiwan." I once played the part of a cunning and cruel spy and drew teeth-grinding denunciations and curses from the audience. For a dress-up program, I appeared as a noble lady, living an easy and pleasant life. This appealed to the female audience, and their faces displayed appreciation and envy. Another time, I danced gracefully in the "Ten Sisters' Fan Dance" so that the audience could enjoy the fancies of the bourgeoisie.

## 17. Learning from the School of Socialism

While working at the Three-Self Movement factory, a leader of the Movement unexpectedly notified me that the provincial government had started a School of Socialism in Sanyuenli in September of 1961. I had been classified as an intellectual and therefore had the opportunity to study there for six months. To be classified as highly intellectual both surprised and delighted me, and I eagerly accepted the opportunity. My Christian colleagues, the Rev. Yip Siu-Hing and Ms. Sung Li-Keen, joined me there, along with the hundred or so other male and female students in the school who were religious leaders, doctors, scientists, university professors, pilots.

Sanyuenli was in the suburbs, where the atmosphere was tranquil and the air, fresh. Our accommodations were first class. Extra helpings were available at every meal. The kitchen staff had purchased a whole flock of plump ducks from the communes, and all kinds of meat were readily available and cheap—only sixty cents renminbi for each dish. The course consisted of morning lectures about national and world affairs from government leaders and famous personalities. Discussion groups were held after the afternoon nap or in the evening, and there was time set aside for reading on our own. Occasionally, arrangements were made for us to visit communes and to share in the fruits of the members' labour—they would proffer plenty of good food for us to try. Through these experiences, we students were to perceive that Socialism was paradise and communes, the ladders to reach it. Our ideology would thereby be changed.

When the air became crisp and the moon was full, when mums were in bloom and fish began to fatten, it was time for our autumn field trip to Chingfai Garden of Daliang in Shundeh. For a few days we enjoyed this enchanting area of elegant estates and quiet gardens, in supreme comfort. A first-class chef was hired to serve us excellent gourmet food. We were provided with a selection of wonderful white bread, exquisite dim-sum, and congee with shredded chicken or chow-mien (stir-fried noodles), just for breakfast. From the hard and frugal life of the communal farm and the factory, I had leaped into luxury inside an ivory tower. This precipitous change made me wonder incredulously whether I had entered heaven-on-earth!

The method of teaching used by the School of Socialism was certainly effective in sowing the impression of the superiority of Socialism. The graduation ceremony was held on the eve of February 1, 1962.

## 18. Joining the History Writing Group

The provincial Political Development Committee leader comrades echoed Premier Chou En-Lai's call and encouraged the older generation to take on the job of writing history. The Premier believed that seniors could best use their leisure time in writing their memoirs so that generations to follow would understand the development of history. The leaders of the provincial Three-Self Movement had formed a History Writing Group in the latter half of 1960. With my agreement, the provincial head of the Religious Affairs department, Mr. Ho Wan, had enrolled me in the group and I became a member.

After the completion of my studies at the School of Socialism, I went every day to the History Data Room on the second floor of the YWCA in Guangzhou. I had the freedom to record any life experience that I deemed of historical value. Often leaders came to deliver speeches on various styles and forms of history writing and on different aspects and viewpoints. The speeches were inspiring and educational.

From the time I joined the History Group until the eve of the Cultural Revolution in August of 1966, I wrote twenty-two articles. Three days before the flame of the Red Guards Movement was lighted, one of the History Group leaders, the Rev. Suen Mo-Shun, conferred with me. He told me that he had already started reading my articles and encouraged me to keep on working. I told him that I planned to channel my efforts into writing a brief history of the South China Diocese of Chunghua Shungkunghui. At the time, the Anglican Diocese of Hong Kong and Macau had just celebrated its centenary and I had access to historical material kept in the History Data Room. It was unthinkable that three days later the Red Guards Movement would begin. And all the gathered data and writings stored in the History Office, all the precious effort and energy of so many of my colleagues over so many years, would be callously turned into ashes.

## 19. The Movement of the Red Guards

On August 25, 1966, at 1 a.m., a group of student Red Guards descended from the rooftop into my third-floor home at Pao Sheng Sha Di Primary School in Shiguan. One of them pushed my right arm with his fist and sent me tumbling and rolling from my bedroom to the living room. Then they challenged me about the source of everything in my home. I responded sarcastically, "They were ripped off from others. Do with them as you please." They forced me to hand over all my jewellery, rings, money, and other precious items. These included a bank account of one hundred and twenty dollars, eighty dollars in cash, a big bowl filled with coins (for bus fare), two ladies' Swiss watches, an emerald jade piece, olive-shaped, nightingale-shaped, gourd-shaped, butterfly-shaped and oval-shaped jade trinkets, a gold-trimmed rattan bracelet, a gold-trimmed jade bracelet, pearls, a pearl tray, a cat's-eye-trimmed diamond ring.

These valuables had been entrusted to my care by my sister-in-law's mother before she passed away. (My brother Ping Yiu and my sister-in-law were living in Britain.) I had been waiting for an opportunity to return them to my sister-in-law. I saw material things as dispensable, so whatever the Red Guards wanted to sweep away as old fashioned, I let them take away. Some China-blue ornaments and lovely items were all taken away. Ostensibly, they were "Sweeping away Four Olds" (ways of thinking, culture, traditions, and bad habits), but in essence, they were looting my home. No matter whether it was morning or night, they came back to plunder more than ten times. Due to the Red Guard's iron fist, my right arm was bruised, swollen, and very painful for a very long time.

Still fresh in my memory is an incident that happened when I was back working in the factory. My pastor neighbour's eldest daughter led the city's Ninth Secondary School Red Guards in breaking into my room. They broke a three-foot-tall, floor-sized antique vase of historical value, which had been treasured for hundreds of years by my sister-in-law's family. Next, they broke a famous vase with a Su Wu shepherding motif and many expensive fine china plates. The gold part of the china stand was broken into pieces. Broken china was all over the kitchen floor. My heart ached to see such national treasures ruined so callously, but I could only swallow my anger and silently move the broken pieces down three flights of stairs to the garbage pile on the street. It took three trips to completely clear them.

Another time, late at night, a group of Red Guards came to my home and ordered me to clear out all the books from three huge bookcases. These were all treasured religious books in both English and Chinese and included my precious Chinese-English Dictionary. The Red Guards put the books into my blanket-cover and mobilized three large carts to move them to the little square of the Zion Church at the west end to be burned. In addition, they burned a lot of shoes and utensils right in the yard of my home.

Still another night, around sixty rascals carrying weapons went straight up to my third-floor home and attempted to rob me and my neighbours. Fortunately, the able-bodied neighbours resisted them on the rooftop. The following night, they came again, and this time the People's Liberation Army came to protect us and we were saved from being hurt. Those rascals spoke with a Hunan accent.

When the Red Guards Movement was just beginning, the Three-Self factory had us clerics go into the yard in front of the YWCA and dig for ammunition. They also made us wear a cardboard sign with "counter-revolutionary cleric" written on it to humiliate us. The most elderly lady of the YWCA, the secretary Chan Shuet-Tung, suffered a severe whipping and was in great pain. They suspected her of knowing of an entrance to an armoury. In truth, the Red Guards had fabricated this rumour and there was no cellar where ammunition was hidden. Only heaven knew the innocent were punished.

The Red Guards used the YWCA buildings as a make-shift prison for the clerics. They burned religious books and Bibles on the grounds in front of the buildings.

## 20. The Cleansing Movement

In the autumn of 1968, a political "Cleansing Movement" unfolded in the province. After the 1966 Cultural Revolution of the proletariat, the Communist Party deepened its search for and uprooting of factions that opposed it. At the same time, efforts to increase the people's loyalty towards Chairman Mao were intensified. During the climax of the movement, students raised placards bearing the character "loyalty" in order to display their ardent loyalty and support for the Chairman.

The "loyalty" placard was rectangular, about four inches wide by five inches high, with a handle of two and a half inches. The large character "loyalty" was decorated with sunflowers on each side. The working class was revered during this movement and entrusted with the leadership of political re-education. These leaders carried extra large loyalty placards. They and their placards led the processions in every event, and they were stationed at conspicuous spots whenever political re-education was held.

Political re-education took place at the Dragon's Eye Cave Reservoir, which was a little distance from Guangzhou. It was a two-hour bus ride north plus an hour's walk away. Along the bank of the reservoir were magnificent villas owned previously by a Shanghai biscuit merchant, Mr. Zao. After the Liberation, the People's government confiscated the property. Here in a garden setting facing the enchanting lake view, the tranquillity and comfort evoked the illusion of being in Shangri-la. The only flaw was that water and electrical facilities had not been installed. People from all walks of life, including religious leaders from among the Catholics, Protestants, Taoists, Buddhists, and Muslims, and the upper class of society in the city, were gathered here to be politically re-educated.

After the San Fan (Three-Anti) Movement of 1951 to 1952, directed against pecuniary corruption, extravagance, and bureaucracy among the urban public civil servants, the city's business sector was rounded up here for ideological re-education. The families of the bourgeoisie were also sent here to keep pigs. Through their pioneering efforts, the foundations of farming and fish-farming were established.

Some of the students at the reservoir could complete their re-education within a year. Others were there for two, three, and even four years before they were free to go home. I was diligent during my labour and re-education program, and remained there for a year, from 1968 to 1969. Every month, I strived to take the four set holidays in order to visit my brother Lee Ching Yiu's wife and my nephew and niece in Guangzhou and enjoy a family gathering.

## Labour

Every morning after breakfast, we students had to perform physical labour. Then after lunch and a brief rest, we gathered in groups to discuss problems and to criticize and learn from each other. Evenings were spent writing reports.

As for physical labour, we were responsible for climbing neighbouring hills and chopping down trees from virgin forests for firewood. There were plenty of trees, but to my dismay, I did not even have the strength to grab a chicken, let alone fell a tree. Fortunately, some male students took pity on me. They bound twelve felled trees into two bunches with thick cord, and then hung the cord around my neck. I pulled these thirty- to forty-foot-long trunks, complete with leaves and branches, down from the hills to the piles in front of the buildings. On my way down, I would be out of breath and my heart would be pounding. During such arduous labour, I often recalled Psalm 121: "I lift up my eyes to the hills—where does my help come from? My help comes from the Lord, and the Maker of heaven and earth."

This strengthened my will and helped me to recover my energy. I could barely complete four round trips of climbing those high hills and pulling trees down the long and tortuous pathways. I would sometimes run into torrential rain, and I had to trek over the muddy and wet hills in my soggy shoes. This caused a lot of suffering for me, an old woman in her sixties. Before a week was out, the leader realized my inadequacy at this type of labour, and sent me to tie up cut grass. Another female student accompanied me and taught me the technique of tying the grass into huge wheel-shaped rolls. These had to be tight in order to roll down the hill. Then the students assigned to work on the boats would transport the wheels of grass to reservoirs, where they were used as provisions for fish.

The reservoir was located beside a highway, and we students were responsible for its protection and maintenance. I was assigned to break up the granite beside the highway into pebbles, which were used to pave the surface before tar was applied. I used a hammer for this, and as time went by, my left thumb and forefinger were hurt. When this task was complete, I was assigned to lighter work—gardening. I pruned, pulled out weeds, added top soil, fertilized, watered, and beautified the potted plants at the villas. This was my chance for rest and enjoyment.

An event occurred during this period of labour that is still etched deeply in my memory. Early one morning, a plump Buddhist monk, Li

Wing-Sau, and I were ordered to cross a bridge to Crab Bay and plant taro. The bridge spanned a deep chasm filled with pebbles and pieces of broken bricks and tiles. The two of us had to carry a basket full of two hundred pounds of taro seeds across that single, narrow plank of a bridge. If we weren't careful, we would certainly fall into the chasm along with the heavy basket. The basket was carried on a long pole between us, which blocked the plank from my view. I could only watch Li Wing-Sau in front of me and follow his footsteps. While I performed this dangerous task, my thoughts could only hang on to my God, who had always been with me, who walked with me, and who had continuously given me strength. Faith was victorious and triumphed over this arduous feat, and we reached our destination of Crab Bay. Faith surely triumphs over all. Hallelujah! God be praised. God is my strength, my song, and my salvation. God's grace is boundless. At the time, I was filled with joy, and I thought of phrases from a poem I had written: "High and low experiences are not worthy of fear / Steadfast Faith will triumph over all."

## *Re-education*

During my year of re-education, I was asked to explain why Bishop Hall of the Anglican Diocese of South China and Hong Kong had broken Anglican tradition and ordained me as the first woman priest.

I had previously encountered questions on this issue. In 1958, a man had unexpectedly visited me at home and had given me a dinner coupon. He told me to have lunch at the Eastern Hotel, and he would meet me there. After lunch, he took me to the Provincial Ministry of Public Safety on a rented tricycle. At the time, I was apprehensive and perturbed. Why was he bringing me here? The man accompanied me to a meeting, where another comrade talked to me and questioned me about my relationship with Bishop Hall. He wanted to know if the Bishop and I had had an intimate relationship, since the Bishop had been willing to break canon law in order to ordain me as the first woman priest. My response to this unexpected and serious question was indignant: "Mrs. Hall is a beautiful and virtuous lady. She and Bishop Hall are known to be in a loving and harmonious marriage. They have smart and healthy children and their family life is happy and blessed. In the church and in the world, Bishop Hall is highly respected as a spiritual and holy bishop. He is prestigious all over the world. How can he possess any desire for me?" The comrade listened to my heartfelt words and was rather taken aback and speechless. So, he let me go.

In the Cleansing Movement re-education class, the above issue was re-introduced as material for criticism and examination. The small group leader cross-examined me concerning my relationship with Bishop Hall. My retort was forthright: "Bishop Hall was my superior at work. His status was holy, and his character, pure. How could he turn from God's love and holiness to take advantage of his subordinate? I am willing to undergo medical tests to prove that I am untainted." As a result of my indignant and severe response, they withdrew. From then on, no one there raised this silly question again.

There was a second matter for which I was criticized. It was the fact that my younger brother, Lee Ching Yui, had stolen his way back to Hong Kong in 1965. I told them I had known nothing beforehand, which was the truth. After he disappeared, we learned from my brother's close friends that he had acted on a rumour that the border was open at Senzhen and so had stolen back to Hong Kong. This left a deep scar in my life. My brother, his wife, their two children, and I had lived as a close-knit family for a long while, and it was a heavy responsibility for me to take care of the two innocent little children while their mother worked. Who would honestly want the only brother they had around, who also happened to be a famous doctor, to be so far away? His search for personal freedom left his family in deep agony. I frankly explained my unsoothable pain to the group members. They all sympathized with me and let me off.

In the re-education group, everyone expressed their opinions and gave oral accounts. However, the last three months at the end of each year were spent writing our autobiographies. Their contents had to be true and patriotic and cover the period of our lives from age fourteen to the present. We started with chronological and light-hearted reports of our life experiences. Next, we wrote about our activities and ideological state of each half year, right up to the current month. We had to list witnesses who would corroborate our statements for each period, so that the leaders could verify our stories.

The last three days before our autobiographies were due were very hectic, as all the lights in dormitories and classrooms were turned off after eleven o'clock at night. Luckily, a female student came up with a bright idea—the two of us made use of the lights in the ladies' washroom. We knelt in front of the toilet, and used its lid as a little desk. After two nights without a wink of sleep, we completed our very detailed autobiographies and handed them in.

After a year of labour and re-education, I was one of the first to be sent back to Guangzhou in 1969. I returned just in time to attend the national celebration on October 1. Within my heart, I praised God unceasingly for his great mercy in allowing me to endure all tests. I could joyfully return to the city to celebrate the nation's birthday. The psalmist said it well: "Taste and see that the Lord is good; blessed is the man who takes refuge in him" (Psa. 34:8); and "The Lord is my light and my salvation."

The labour and re-education during my stay at the reservoir were very enervating. Nevertheless, the provisions had been abundant. Every meal was sumptuous. Often, fish caught fresh from the reservoir were served. Some were "big heads," weighing fifteen pounds and upwards. They were right from the nets and were fresh and tasty. Meat was plenteous, for the fattened pigs reared in the compound were often slaughtered for our consumption. We also had vegetables from our fields. There were even snacks after night classes. The pork congee and sushi could satisfy any glutton.

## 21. Retirement from the Factory

On July 1, 1974, leaders at the Forward factory decided to encourage elderly workers to retire. There were ten such, and I was among them, having worked there off and on since 1966. After we had left the factory, the Three-Self Movement Committee gave twenty renminbi to each person every month as living allowance. What follows is a brief description of my life after retirement.

### *Serious Eye Trouble*

July 1 is the anniversary of the Chinese Communist Party, and it was celebrated with a public holiday in Guangzhou. My first day of retirement fell on that day, and I was happy to go swimming with a few friends at nearby Sanyuenli Springs. The water was very crowded with people and, unfortunately, I contracted an eye infection that developed into conjunctivitis (pink eye disease). I was treated by ophthalmologist Dr. Yeung Yee-Kar of the People's First City Hospital. However, a prolonged eye ailment gradually reduced my sight until 1978 when a caring parishioner recommended that I see Dr. Chan Lin Oi, the chief ophthalmologist at Guangzhou Eye Hospital. As soon as the specialist saw me, she recognized me as her former teacher at the Guangzhou Union Girls' Secondary School. She took great care in examining me and personally operated on my eye to cure my long-suffering problem of ingrown eyelashes. I felt deep gladness, thinking of our Lord Jesus healing the blind when He walked on earth. He said, "The eye is the lamp of the body. If your eyes are good, your whole body will be full of light" (Matt. 6:22). The writer of Proverbs said, "Guard my teachings as the apple of your eye" (Prov. 7:2). Our vision is more important than our sight. Lord Jesus is the true light of the world. How important it is to live in Him!

## *Diligently Practising Kung Fu*

I was earnest in maintaining my physical strength after my retirement. Since I had the leisure, and my home was near quiet Laichee Wan Pond, every morning I met with some friends at the Pond park to learn taichi and taichi sword art from a master. I did that for three years.

The rest of my time was scheduled to be spent on the Three-Self Movement Association's political, current affairs, and international affairs classes. Whenever I had a chance, I would visit my sister-in-law and help care for my niece and nephew. My niece Sze-Sze responded to the Farm Communal Program for Young Intellectuals and had worked in Pok-law for two years, in 1976 and 1977. Afterwards, she successfully passed the Weiyang city matriculation and entered Guangzhou Chungshan University faculty of English to study. My nephew Sze-Wing was an electronics apprentice in a factory.

## *Teaching English*

In 1979, China opened its doors and foreign relations became important. I was recruited to welcome foreign guests. At that time, English teachers were scarce, so a list of names of potential teachers was drawn up. My name was on the list. More than ten post-secondary educational institutions urgently wanted English teachers.

A leader of the Army Medical School came twice to my home to try and persuade me to go and help out army personnel. This group of personnel was soon to be sent abroad to study. They needed a general knowledge of foreign lifestyles and a familiarity with common English expressions. The medical school offered a good salary and daily transportation there and back. At that time, my eye condition was still serious, and I used it as an excuse to decline. In fact I was afraid that, if I obeyed them, I would open myself up to criticism in the event of further political movements. Someone might accuse me of audaciously sneaking into military institutions to attempt counter-revolutionary activities. Also, if church activities were revived one day, my being tied up with teaching would conflict with my primal wish to serve God with my whole life.

I therefore resolved to teach English to my niece Sze-Sze English in order to prepare her for her matriculation. I also used my free time to tutor children of my fellow church workers in English in case they wanted to go abroad to study. I used fundamental English textbooks for secondary schools as teaching material. As a result, the two daughters of a co-worker had the opportunity to study abroad. My niece was accepted into the faculty of English of Guangzhou Chungshan University and received her bachelors' degree in 1982. She later furthered her studies in Switzerland and Canada.

## 22. My Financial Situation

When the Red Guards Movement began in the latter half of August 1966, the church had officially ceased all activities, and its assets were frozen. Salaries for clergy were suspended.

During the time between August 1966, when I started work at the Forward factory, and January of 1974, I received twelve renminbi a month in living allowance. In January, my living allowance was raised to twenty-six renminbi per month, and in April, it was further increased to thirty-two renminbi until July of that year, when I retired.

When church activities revived in 1979, clergy had not received their original salary for a period of fourteen years. My monthly salary had originally been one hundred renminbi. In 1980, when the church's frozen assets were released, the Three-Self Movement proceeded to compensate clergy with back-pay in three instalments, after first deducting our living allowance from our original salaries.

## 23. Religious Freedom Restored

On the eve of our national celebration in 1979, the government declared religious freedom. The Patriotic Three-Self Movement raised its flag again. In November of that year, churches restored their Sunday worship and religious services. According to the report of the Fourth Annual

National Christian Conference in 1986, four thousand churches around the nation were reopened. Thirty-three ministers were ordained and a sixth of them were women.

In Guangdong Province, only Tunshan Church in Guangzhou was available for worship. Even though it was dingy, dilapidated, and in need of re-consecration of the altar, we celebrated our Christmas there. That Christmas celebration is one I have never forgotten.

In a country in dire need of material goods, we couldn't celebrate it in the traditional way. We had no Christmas tree, or decorative sets of shepherds and wise men at the stable. There was no Santa Claus to give out presents to the children. Even the liturgy of Holy Eucharist had to be abbreviated, not to mention the joy of fellowship of a Christmas dinner for parishioners. However, we could and did hold a solemn Christmas thanksgiving service. More than twenty young people joined together to form a choir. And although their surplices were not ready, hearing the message of the birth of our Saviour in beautiful song deeply moved the congregation of over a thousand. Their praises and thanksgiving echoed in unison. The reverberation of the carols could be heard in east Guangzhou.

I was deeply touched. This Christmas celebration was a reminder of the complexity of human relations and how important the birth of Christ was to humanity. Consider the years of the Cultural Revolution, for example, in which material things were destroyed, human dignity was trampled, lives were sacrificed, and condemnation was suffered by the innocent—who can pass fair judgement on who was responsible and who was at fault?

We are fortunate to have the birth of Christ Jesus, who gave up himself to save mankind. This great sacrifice of life by the righteous for the iniquitous shows that "God demonstrates his own love for us in this: While we were still sinners, Christ died for us" (Rom. 5:8). St Peter said, "Love covers over a multitude of sins." The Lord asserted the principle of forgiveness everywhere. While nailed on the cross, He continued to pray for God's forgiveness of those who were responsible, for they did not know what they were doing.

If we base our actions on secular principles, then vengeance upon vengeance will never end. Christ was born as the Prince of Peace, just as St Paul said: "Christ came to spread the gospel of peace to those near and far." Christ came, as Word became flesh. The highest purpose was to realize "on earth as in heaven": for all wars to cease, to maintain world peace, obliterate man-made woes, promote human peaceful co-existence and harmony, and create an ideal world together with God.

# Part Three
# *1981–1985*

✤ ✤ ✤

## 24. My Application to Visit Relatives Abroad

I was the only one of my immediate family who still remained in China. The others were all living overseas at that time, in Hong Kong, England, Switzerland, and Canada. For many years they had hoped that I could visit them for a family reunion, and enjoy a trip abroad in the evening of my life. After I retired from the factory, they pressed me even more urgently to apply for an exit visa. My nephew Li Tak-Kut in Canada had applied on my behalf to the Immigration Department in 1974. After a seven-year wait, I was granted a visa to visit overseas for a year. I had received two instalments of back pay from the Three-Self Movement. So, in November 1981, I made plans to visit my overseas relatives and return.

## 25. My Stay in Hong Kong

My niece Sze-Kit took me shopping for items I would need for travelling and made arrangements for my stay in Hong Kong. In addition, she arranged for a tea party at the Ling-Nam University Alumni Restaurant so I could meet with my long-separated friends and say good-bye to them. Over fifty of my friends were there, including Miss Wong Yuk-Miu, retired General Secretary of the Hong Kong YWCA, Sung Kam-Ping, the Rev. Tsang Kai-Choi, the Rev. Canon Cheung Luk-Heung, and the Ven. Pang Wing-Cheong. I was also invited to attend the tenth anniversary celebration of the ordination of the Revs. Joyce Bennett and Jane Huang, where I celebrated Eucharist and preached. The staff and students of St Catherine's Girls' School also came to praise and offer thanksgiving.

The Revs. Bennett and Huang were ordained twenty-seven years after my own ordination. The ordination of these two women priests made me feel that I was not fighting alone, and intensified my faith in my ministry. The Rev. Li Ching-Chi, female minister of the Christian Church in China, also came to this gathering to offer praise and thanksgiving with the permission of the Rev. Peter Wong. Five women priests of the Anglican Church, Joyce Bennett, Jane Huang, Mary Au, Shek Wing-Sheut, and I, got together for a precious photograph.

After a week in Hong Kong, I flew to Canada in the company of my brother Hon-Yiu's wife, Cheng Po-Kuen, their daughter Vivian, and grand-daughter Tseng Pui-Chi.

## 26. Activities Abroad

### Family Gathering in Canada

At last, I could experience the joy of a family reunion. The inner bliss was difficult to describe, but I wrote a poem to release my feelings:

> Affinity of old had only deepened
> through thirty years of parting.
> What a lark to gather one's own flesh and blood,
> unified in joy everlasting.

### The Days in Montreal

I reached Montreal, Canada, on 2 December, 1981, and stayed at the home of my niece Vivian and her husband Ronald Tseng. At that time, she had just given birth to their second daughter, and I helped her to care for her first born, Pui-Chi. This little girl loved the clay animals I made, cows, sheep, horses, giraffes, cats, and dogs. Sometimes I crayoned pictures of the sun, moon, and stars, flowers and meadows, while she watched with absorbed interest.

At Christmas, Vivian invited friends and relatives to a Christmas party at her home. We had a worship service under the shimmering lights of the Christmas tree. I led in the worship and delivered the homily entitled "the shepherds on Christmas night." I encouraged the audience to follow the example of the shepherds, who heard the heralding angels, went to Bethlehem to worship the Christ-child, and joyfully spread the word, for we also have the responsibility of spreading the gospel of salvation. When worship was over, we had a pot-luck dinner. My brother and his wife brought a roasted suckling pig and everyone had a good time.

On Christmas day, Vivian took me to St George's Anglican Church for Christmas Eucharist. The rector, the Rev. Canon Cleator, welcomed us warmly. In the afternoon, we attended the Christmas service of the Chinese Alliance Church and the sumptuous high tea held afterwards.

While in Montreal, I followed Vivian's family on a trip to the snow-covered mountain of St Bruno and wrote a poem to describe the fun:

> It was a beautiful sunny day.
> Seeing the crystal-veiled trees
> and squirrels playing on the silvery landscape
> filled my heart with glee.

## *The Baptism of Pui-Shan*

Vivian's second daughter, Pui-Shan, had been born on April 14, 1982. On May 16, she was baptised by the Rev. Canon Cleator at St George's Anglican Church. It was a celebrated event among friends and relatives, and many pictures were taken. I was invited to read three lessons during worship. That evening, the "full month" celebration of the baby was held at Montreal's Peninsular Restaurant, and it was a joyful event.

After his retirement, my youngest brother Hon-Yiu emigrated from Hong Kong to Canada on May 3, 1982, just in time for his granddaughter Pui-Shan's baptism. That summer, on July 10, his entire family and I visited the Thousand Islands on vacation.

## 27. Settling Down in Toronto

After my brother Hon-Yiu and his wife came to Canada, they left the beautiful and cultured city of Montreal in November to move to suburban Toronto. I left my niece's home and moved with them.

Although I had come to Canada as a visitor, my relatives had begged me to stay on. Their reason was that I was almost an octogenarian. If I insisted on going back to China, no one could look after me. So I sent in my application for emigration. After two years, China granted me permission to emigrate due to my situation, and I became a Canadian immigrant.

Once in Toronto, I was fortunate to have the loving concern of the Rev. Kenneth Fung of Toronto's St John's Chinese Congregation and St Matthew's Anglican Church, and the permission of Bishop Parke-Taylor to do my part there to spread the gospel.

## 28. The Fortieth Ordination Anniversary Celebration in Toronto

On January 14, 1984, St John's Chinese Congregation held a Thanksgiving Eucharist. Over two hundred were in attendance. The Archbishop of Canada, the Most Rev. Ted Scott, delivered the sermon. He highly commended the late Bishop R. O. Hall's sagacity, decisiveness, and courage in authorizing my ordination and becoming an avant garde in the Movement for the Ordination of Women.

At the service, I celebrated Eucharist while the Revs. Ken Fung and Alison Kemper assisted. Suffragan Bishop Parke-Taylor gave the benediction. Priests from the Japanese and Korean Anglican Churches and two Canadian women priests also took part in the service. My sister Rita read the Epistle. After the service, a twelve-table banquet was held at a nearby Chinese restaurant in honour of my fortieth ordination anniversary. It was an exciting event, and all who were present were united in their offer of praises to God. Many clergy members delivered speeches of congratulations and gave me much encouragement. I was deeply touched.

### *My Speech at the Celebration*

"Today, on January 14, 1984, St Matthew's and St John's are hosting a dinner in honour of the fortieth anniversary of my ordination to the priesthood. I thank God from the bottom of my heart that I am able to share in this happy fellowship and to praise God for His blessings. It is indeed a rare and treasured moment.

"I wish to thank Bishop Parke-Taylor, the Rev. Fung, and the curate, the Rev. Alison Kemper, and all of you for the thanksgiving service and dinner party. I am especially grateful for the alb you have given me—an alb embroidered with a cross. I am deeply moved by the importance that all of you have placed on my fortieth ordination anniversary, and such an elaborate celebration was totally beyond my expectations. I am very grateful for the precious time, energy, spirit, and materials you have given towards this thanksgiving event of fellowship, which is blooming with joy and harmony. Your happy hearts amply show the greatness of God's blessings. May God be glorified.

"By the grace of God, I have been serving the church ever since I was ordained. Throughout these forty years, I have experienced many severe tests, such as the Sino-Japanese war, and the turmoil it brought, then the fighting of China's Liberation, the proletariat Cultural Revolution, and the chain of various political movements. Fortunately, God was with me every moment. Whenever I was face to face with peril, His gracious hand held me fast and led me onwards to overcome countless obstacles. The psalmist said it well: "Even though I walked through the valley of the shadow of death, I fear no evil, for you are with me; your rod and your staff, they comfort me" (Psa. 23:4). How true and sweet is the taste of God's mercy.

"Shortly after my ordination to priesthood, I felt the pressure of opposition from the conservative Church of England leaders who were against the ordination of women. However, through the strength and comfort given by God, I took that in stride and persevered happily at my post in the church for many decades, as if in a day.

"I am happy to tell you that I am not the sole female Anglican priest today. The second group of women were ordained twenty-seven years after my ordination. In 1971, the Diocese of Hong Kong ordained Joyce Bennett and Jane Huang as priests. At the present time, 660 female priests have been ordained throughout the world. Only 660 women have been ordained priests in forty years. This movement is not progressing fast enough. Today's trend indicates that more and more women want to commit themselves to serving the Lord. In Britain, nineteen women are now ready to be ordained priests. Unfortunately, Britain is still in a conservative stage.

"In preparation for my ordination anniversary, I have had an opportunity to examine and assess my work so far. I have discovered my many weaknesses, and it was God's mercy that I was continually renewed in order to keep on witnessing for Him.

"I pray that God will overlook my inadequacies, and through your love and encouragement, and the life, health, and peaceful opportunities bestowed by God, I hope to finish the task with which God has entrusted me with all my heart, all my soul, all my mind, and all my strength, during the remainder of my life. With every one of you, I will raise up the light of salvation of the cross and live the gospel!"

Here is an excerpt from St John's Voice No. 3, which I wrote concerning the events on the day of the fortieth anniversary celebration:

"January 1984 was the fortieth anniversary of my ordination to priesthood. I am grateful to my brothers and sisters in Christ and my clergy colleagues for celebrating this event in Toronto, Canada, and in London and Sheffield in England. I am a very minor and unimportant person. To be so honoured through the blessing of God moves and humbles me. I can only work hard for the Lord and do my best for the rest of my days in order to glorify Him and benefit people. I am writing a record of the celebrations and my reflections to alert myself and to aid in remembrance."

## 29. The Celebration in England

I left Toronto for London, England, on January 19 in order to attend the grand thanksgiving celebration in Westminster Abbey. However, from the time of my arrival, there were a host of activities. As soon as I arrived on the twentieth, Dean Alan Webster of St Paul's Cathedral led me on a tour of the church building and its precious collection of vestments, communion vessels, and altar decorations. These treasures were of great historical value and were very splendid.

### *Celebration at Westminster Abbey*

The thanksgiving service at Westminster Abbey was held on January 21. It began with an anthem by the choir, which comprised the entire faculty and students of the University Church of Christ the King, London. Over a hundred deaconesses from all over Britain, tens of licensed lay readers, fifteen overseas women priests, eleven bishops, and all the clergy of Westminster Abbey were in attendance, over three hundred in all. After the dolcet and beautiful music, this huge procession of flowing gowns entered the church with solemn steps and gladsome hearts. Former Bishop of Hong Kong and Macau Bishop Gilbert Baker celebrated the Eucharist, and all the female clergy assisted. The Rev. Joyce Bennett, who had returned to England after her retirement, preached. Over a thousand in the congregation rejoiced in thanksgiving.

On the day before the service at Westminster Abbey, the Archbishop of Canterbury, Dr. Robert Runcie, had sent me a greeting. This was read out loud during the ceremony. He wrote that he held my work in high esteem and he praised my perseverance. He said that, unperturbed by the church's opposition to the ordination of women priests, I had quietly devoted myself to serving the church without self-promotion and thus had set an example to others. This letter won a lengthy round of applause from the congregation.

Later that day, a banquet was held at the Chinese Anglican Congregation of St Martin (-in-the-Fields). Due to limited seating, attendance was limited to around three hundred persons. Afterwards, over four hundred people gathered on the steps outside the church to raise a torch and sing hymns. This was done in hopes that the blazing fire could blaze a path of equality for men and women through the obstinacy of the church, the same right to serve the church could be enjoyed by all. The celebration ended with fireworks, which boomed and bloomed in the clear night sky and shook the entire city of London.

## *A Visit with Friends*

On the twenty-fourth, I was invited by the Rev. Bennett's Aunt Emily to have lunch at her home. Even though she was in her nineties, her hospitality was commendable. She introduced me to traditional English etiquette, which allowed me to see the way English Christian families lived. The next day, the twenty-fifth, was my ordination anniversary. At eight in the morning, a friend drove the Rev. Bennett and me to the Church of St Peter's and St Paul's for communion with Bishop Simon of Buckingham as celebrant. The church loomed high on a hill, with a scenic view of the surrounding valley.

Now that I was in England, I seized the opportunity to visit Mrs. Geoffrey Allen, wife of the Rev. Geoffrey Allen. When I was a theological student, I had been much impressed by the Rev. Allen, a New Testament professor. Both he and his wife had been very kind to me, and he hailed me as "his beloved student" in the letters he wrote to me. After the Sino-Japanese war, Professor Allen was consecrated Bishop of Cairo and later became Bishop of Derby after he had returned to England. They also loved Bishop Ronald Hall's son, the Rev. Canon Christopher Hall, very much and named him as the beneficiary of their estate in Mrs. Allen's will.

On January 26, I was invited to lunch with her, together with the Rev. Bennett. Host and guests had a hearty chat, and we were all thankful and happy for the chance to meet again.

## The Door to Westminster Abbey Was Opened

According to the *London Church Times* of January 27, 1984, "Westminster Abbey, more accustomed to grand occasions of State and to saluting poets and national heroes, bent its majesty instead to the honouring of a 'mere worm'—Miss Li's own description of herself." As the recipient of such honour, how could I be unmoved? Yet my enjoyment of such glory alerted me. I asked myself how a person as weak as myself could be worthy of such honour. I could only bow my head in penitence and earnest prayer, and go through a thorough spiritual ablution. Like St Paul, I would not hide my weaknesses but let the power of Christ protect me and His blood cleanse me. I would adopt the attitude of "let bygones be bygones" and hold on to the promise, "I am making everything new!" (Rev. 21:5). I would work even harder at spreading the gospel and the truth for the remainder of my life.

## Celebration in Sheffield

Sheffield is in the northern part of England. When the celebration in London was over, I went on to Yorkshire to attend the thanksgiving service at the Sheffield cathedral on January 28. The preacher and celebrant was Canon Christopher Hall, son of the late Bishop R. O. Hall. He invited me to assist him during Eucharist. There were over three hundred in the congregation for the service, and the order of service itself was very creative. Using the Old Testament story of Jonah in dialogue form as background, it expressed my obedience to God's commission to spread the gospel and proclaim that God wanted us to repent and those who did would be forgiven.

After tea, the congregation gathered at the church hall to watch a marvellous skit that mocked the conservative church leaders who were against the ordination of women to priesthood. In reality, Anglican Churches outside of Britain had already ordained 660 women priests. These women had borne great responsibilities and achieved wonderful results. The skit was an outstanding and interesting performance. It was comical, but sarcastic, and the audience was stirred.

## Lambeth Meeting

In the afternoon of February 7, accompanied by Bishop Gilbert Baker and the Rev. Joyce Bennett, I accepted Dr. Runcie's invitation to visit him at Lambeth Palace. He was amiable and kind, gentle and meek. We had a heart-to-heart talk. He expressed his personal sympathy and support concerning the issue of ordination of women priests in Britain. However, the Church of England had a long tradition and strict canon laws that could not be changed overnight. It would take time and close examination in order to achieve understanding; haste would only hamper progress. He took my hands affectionately in his and prayed that God would bestow me with countless blessings. Lastly, he bid me sincerely to pray for him so that God would increase his ability and wisdom to handle this difficult case of ordaining women priests.

I was enthralled to personally hear this wish and charge for me from such a highly spiritual, experienced, erudite, and revered church leader. All the joy, honour, and blessings I had received were, not only to hearten me so I would not be discouraged by the flaws of my past, but to incite me to be vigilant through the flickering flame of my God-given life, and fight with time to compensate for them. Moreover, I realized that I had been using my age as an excuse to beat the receding drum and it was time to stop counting my years. The psalmist's prayer shimmered in my mind: "Even when I am old and grey / Do not forsake me, O God / till I declare your power to the next generation / your might to all who are to come" (Psa. 71:18).

After our visit with Dr. Runcie, Bishop Baker took me to Dean Webster's residence for lunch. Then, Bishop Baker invited us home to meet Mrs. Baker. We went to Eucharist at St Martin's next morning and had lunch at Bishop Baker's, together with Mr. and Mrs. Bob Whyte.

## *The Movement for the Ordination of Women in England*

The Movement for the Ordination of Women in England was just developing fervour. The goal of the Movement was for all women who accepted God's call to serve the church full time to be ordained as priests, just as men were. As I was the first woman priest ordained in the Anglican Communion, my fortieth ordination anniversary served as strong testimony for the cause and encouragement for the Movement.

Meanwhile, the Church of England was maintaining its conservative position, using rigid and outdated canons to deter those women devout in serving the kingdom of heaven from expressing their talents to the fullest. What a pity it was! Religious canons, orders, and systems are all man-made. As Christians, we should understand God's will. God created both male and female, and we are all His children. He surely wants His children to work with each other and support each other in making "heaven on earth" a reality. Why are there unenlightened, intransigent, and obstinate people who want to strip away women's freedom to serve the Lord, and suppress their work? Could that be in accordance with Christ's teachings? In the Gospel of John, 8:32, Jesus says, "You will know the truth, and the truth will set you free." Can there be truth in suppressing women who love God and want to serve Him?

When Christ walked on earth, He respected women everywhere, and there are countless examples of how women served Him devotedly. Martha and Mary both served the Lord, and the Lord was pleased with them, saying, "Mary has chosen what is better, and it will not be taken away from her." Then there was the woman who anointed Jesus with perfume. Even though she was rebuked by others, Jesus treasured her action as "a beautiful thing," saying, "wherever the gospel is preached throughout the world, what she has done will also be told, in memory of her." After His resurrection, Jesus appeared first to Mary Magdalene, Joanna, Mary, the mother of James, and the other women with them.

Christ Jesus respected and esteemed the service of women. How can the die-hard leaders of the Church of England hide their heads in the sand and ignore and suppress the rights of the women who serve the church? When the apostles were being persecuted, Gamaliel, who was honoured by all the people, said, "Leave these men alone! Let them go! For if their purpose or activity is of human origin, it will fail. But if it is from God, you will not be able to stop these men; you will only find yourselves fighting against God" (Acts 5). Let me audaciously ask: Is keeping qualified English women from ordination to priesthood in accordance to God's will? Or is it fighting against God's great plan?

## *In Conclusion*

I felt flattered and overwhelmed to attend the thanksgiving services in England in honour of the fortieth anniversary of my ordination. Other than these great events, there were many other gatherings and celebrations where questions were asked and answers sought, and where deep feelings were shared. I was nourished in my spiritual growth and in the exchange of experiences. They were truly exceptional and meaningful encounters. From these, I felt deeply my past inadequacies in spreading the gospel and furthering the kingdom of heaven.

Now that I had been so uplifted, I could only put my hand to the plough and never look back. Ample opportunities to serve God were waiting ahead, for it was the time when "the harvest is plentiful but the workers are few" (Luke 10:2). Even though I could say that I had experienced some small achievements in the past, this was only so because God had used me, and I had nothing of which to boast. The Lord Jesus taught us that "when you have done everything you were told to do, you should say, 'We are unworthy servants; we have only done our duty'" (Luke 17:10). Those three weeks in England bestowed upon me by God were an opportunity to deepen my knowledge, an opportunity to receive challenge and encouragement. These opportunities were as described in Ephesians 3:20: "Him who is able to do immeasurably more than all we ask or imagine, according to his power that is at work within us." From the bottom of my heart and the depth of my soul, I sincerely extol, "To him who sits on the throne and to the Lamb be praise and honour and glory and power, for ever and ever!" (Rev. 5:13).

## 30. Travelling to Geneva, Rome, and Paris

On February 9, 1984, I flew from London and arrived safely in Geneva. I had long dreamed of touring this world-famous, beautiful garden city. In my excitement, I could only thank God from the bottom of my heart, and praise Him for His blessings. The day after my arrival, I visited the grave of my sister Rita's late husband, Lee Yen-Ping. Yen-Ping's tombstone was huge, a dark yet glossy grey marble. It was elegant and beautiful. I later told Rita never to move his grave. In my opinion, he had chosen his eternal place of rest. May his soul be in heaven, and his body be at his resting place, and his joy everlasting. The next time I visited there, I proffered fresh flowers in respect.

I had heard that Rita had a "country villa." Eager to see it for myself, I visited her in the country on the third day after my arrival. The building materials used in the villa were very sturdy, and its foundation was formed of granite. The inside was spacious, consisting of two connecting two-story buildings. The garden was extensive and included some fruit trees, emerald bamboo, and a profusion of roses. It was truly an elegant villa for rest and leisure.

On Monday, February 13, I attended a staff luncheon of the World Council of Churches and delivered a short talk. I introduced the audience to the developments of the Chinese Church's Three-Self Movement, its strong faith and increasing membership, and the freedom to worship it now enjoyed. I also visited the new building of the International Labour Office. Its huge pillars were very majestic.

On February 14, Rita tried to get me a travel visa to go to Paris, France, and we spent a whole day doing just that. On the fifteenth, at 9:45 a.m., a friend, "White Bear," took the two of us to the airport to board the 10:45 flight bound for Rome. We arrived at our destination at 1:45 p.m. and enjoyed a bus tour around the Colosseum, St Peter's Basilica, the Forum, and other tourist attractions. The next morning, we were on our way to the Vatican. Unfortunately, we did not have a chance to meet Pope John Paul II.

In the afternoon, we visited museums in the Vatican, St Peter's Basilica, the Sistine Chapel, and St Peter's tomb, where we knelt down to pray in the cellar. There, we met Archbishop Glem of Poland. Rita greeted him and spoke with him for a while. Rita had taken a vacation in Poland, and her friends, a Polish couple who were both university professors, were very hospitable and excellent tour guides.

We also got to see the Catacombs after dealing with traffic problems. This dark page in history reflects the vestiges of the cruel persecution of Christians by the Roman Empire. At the same time, it pays tribute to those brave Christians who understood that the body could be slain, but the soul, through stalwart faith, could never be hurt.

On February 19, we arrived in Paris. That evening, we had dinner at the Hey-Hing Restaurant. The proprietors, Mr. and Mrs. Leung Ching-Wah, had been good friends with Rita since Mr. Leung's business days in Geneva. The Leungs greeted us at the door, and led us to a private dining room. Mrs. Leung herself prepared a delicious menu of steamed sole, stir-fried prawns, and other delicacies. It was wonderful to enjoy Cantonese food while we were travelling abroad, and we will never forget Mr. and Mrs. Leung's hospitality.

The next day, we arose early and toured the army museum, Napoleon's Tomb, and Le Louvre. Of the many famous paintings in the Louvre, we could only sample a few. The painting I enjoyed the most was *Mona Lisa* by Leonardo da Vinci. The natural beauty and serene poise of the portrait captivated me. How marvellous is the stroke of an artist's brush!

As we could only stay in Paris for two days, we took a train to Palais de Versailles on the twenty-second. Countless ornate and sparkling crystal chandeliers hung in the palace. The First World War peace treaty was signed there and the tiding of peace spread jubilantly to every corner of the earth. It meant so much to me to visit this place! The next day, we took the Metro to visit Notre Dame. Next, we hurried to L'arch de Triumph, and from its vantage point, meditated on the glorious result of Napoleon's revolution and stood in tribute.

## 31. Back to Toronto

On February 27, 1984, I flew from Geneva to London and transferred back to Toronto. Upon my arrival, my niece Sze-Sze and my brother Hon-Yiu came to the airport to greet me, which gave me great comfort. The next morning, on the twenty-eighth, there was a snowstorm.

On Ash Wednesday, March 7, I met with a Toronto reporter from *The Globe and Mail*. Mr. Stan Oziewiez and his wife had visited China in 1981. Mr. Oziewiez was interested in my life story and my ordination, and wanted to hear about my recent trip to Geneva. I gave him British newspaper clippings of my fortieth ordination anniversary celebrations in England. That morning, a photographer took pictures of me in my vestments celebrating Eucharist at my parish.

Mr. Ted Harrison, a reporter from the British Broadcasting Corporation, flew to Toronto from England on May 27 to meet with me in person. For a whole week, he talked with me about my life, my work, and my experiences. He asked thoughtful and penetrating questions concerning my commitment to serving the Lord and the events around my ordination to priesthood. He gathered this information into a short biography of me, which was published by Darton, Longman & Todd in England. The book was entitled *Much Beloved Daughter*.

On May 1 of 1984, the Rev. Ken Fung was transferred from St John's Chinese Congregation to All Saints' Chinese Church in Scarborough and the Rev. Lau Wan served as interim priest for St John's until July 15. On August 16, the Rev. Edmund Der of Hong Kong took up the post and was inducted on October 13, when the parish was celebrating its anniversary. I am very thankful that I was able to serve the church as honorary assistant with the above-mentioned priests. I have shared in their rich experiences and their merits in managing the parish. This is a miracle of God's blessing.

## 32. Joining a Pilgrimage to Jerusalem

My sister Rita understood what serving the Lord meant to me and she was an ardent supporter of my work. She often confided to me that she wondered how I, as a member of the clergy, could lead a congregation to a deeper knowledge of Jesus, to a stalwart faith through the crucifixion story, without having been on a pilgrimage to Jerusalem. She thought I needed to walk the hills, plains, deserts, and rivers that Jesus had walked. She was determined that I make a trip to Jerusalem, and through the recommendation of the Rev. Christopher Hall, the closing of 1984 saw the two of us joining a pilgrimage tour organized by the Diocese of Sheffield of England. We were escorted by Canon Bostock for our ten days of pious living.

Jerusalem, with its more than four thousand years of history, is the Holy Land of God's only Son, incarnate, our Saviour Jesus Christ. In Jerusalem, we visited monuments every day and I learned a lot.

On the day we arrived, I strolled about after supper in Old Jerusalem, the Holy City. The ancient streets were narrow and dim, paved with broken bricks and cobblestones, rugged and rough. During the day, hawkers lined their wares along both sides of the streets and transformed the area into a busy marketplace.

We first toured the church that commemorated Christ's Ascension. A large rock lay in a fenced-off area, and on the rock was a legendary footprint of Christ. We immediately and reverently touched the rock to show devotion towards Christ.

After exiting this church, we walked towards the Mount of Olives and reached The Church of Dominus Flevit. Canon Bostock, our leader, gave us Holy Communion there to deepen our sense of being with the Lord. On a marble piece in front of the altar was an etching of Jesus grieving over Jerusalem, saying, "How often have I longed to gather your children together, as a hen gathers her chicks under her wings, but you were not willing." Behind the altar was an eye-shaped window. From this window, we could see the Temple Square and the monumental Dome of the Rock, with its glittering golden top.

The next day, we saw the Garden of Gethsemane, which consisted of elegant and serene olive groves and ostentatious blossoms. This lovely environment naturally elicited the image of Jesus encouraging His disciples to keep watch with Him. The Lord went a little further and fell with His face to the ground and prayed, "My Father, if it is possible, may this cup be taken from me. Yet not as I will, but as you will." Canon Bostock stood close to us, and together we recited Matthew 26:36-39, followed by meditation. He then led us in prayer and bid us to consider, "Yet not as I will, but as you will." This experience served as a lesson in obedience to God's will. Gethsemane is also the place where Jesus was betrayed and arrested (Luke 23:47-53). Our visit here deepened our appreciation of Christ's suffering and sacrifice for our sins, and enlivened our ardent love for the Lord.

There were huge and ancient trees in the garden. Some had been growing for over a thousand years. Others had been growing since the day of Jesus's arrest, and were over two thousand years old. Other trees in the garden were progeny of these ancient olive trees. It was said that after the dead branches of olive trees are pruned, new shoots will grow and yield even more fruit. The various and delicious olive products we enjoyed at breakfast each day in the Holy City gave proof to this adage.

Later, we entered Herod's Gate, which leads to the remains of Herod's Palace. Herod presided over the trial of Jesus in this place (Luke 23:13-17), but found no basis for a charge against Him. Jesus was indeed righteous and died for the unrighteous.

We also viewed the Holy Sepulchre. This was erected by Emperor Constantine in 325 AD, on the site of the last of the five stations on Christ's way to Golgotha where he was crucified. According to tradition, it was also the tomb where Jesus' body was placed after it was taken down from the cross. The Holy Sepulchre was built to commemorate the death and resurrection of Jesus.

Next, we visited the Wailing Wall, which is also called the West Wall. From the entrance, Dung Gate, the old Jerusalem city wall can be seen. The Jewish people wail at the Wailing Wall because their original temple was destroyed and the Ark of Covenant lost. They are still waiting for the Messiah to come, and reject Jesus as the Messiah. They hope to recover the Ark; therefore, they still cry at the Wailing Wall. The Wall is separated into two sections, with a partition in between. Males stand on the left side, and females, on the right. All who visit read the Bible and pray out loud. They write little notes and place them in the cracks of the Wailing Wall as a way of sending messages to God.

In the square behind the Wailing Wall stands a domed temple, built on the rock. It stands on the site of the original temple from which Jesus drove out all who were buying and selling and overturned the tables of the money-changers. He taught them, "Is it not written, 'My house will be called a house of prayer for all nations'? But you have made it 'a den of robbers'" (Mark 11:15-17). According to tradition, the rock is the altar upon which Abraham was to sacrifice his son Isaac in obedience to God. The Dome itself is made of gold. In the sun, it glittered majestically and glamorously, lustrous and attractive. From the inside, the dome is a beautiful mosaic of sparkling gems, its craftsmanship outstanding. Believers turned their devotion and respect for God into marvellous and creative works of art. Their sacrifices to God and their piety were applaudable.

On the last day of our pilgrimage, we crossed the Sea of Galilee and reached the River Jordan before dusk. Canon Bostock sprinkled water in a re-enactment of Jesus' baptism by John the Baptist in the River Jordan, when Jesus heard a voice from heaven saying, "This is my Son, whom I love; with him I am well pleased" (Matt. 3:17). During this ceremony, I deeply appreciated the intimate relationship between the Father and the Son and was much elated.

## 33. Another Journey to Europe

On January 9, 1985, Rita and I flew from Tel Aviv to Geneva through Zurich. We stayed in Geneva for almost two weeks and afterwards toured around Austria, Italy, Switzerland, Brussels in Belgium, and the Netherlands. We set off for the Austrian capital of Vienna on the morning of January 22. The train passed through very scenic areas, and the untainted snow added to the splendour. As we were riding First Class, our travels were all the more enjoyable.

On our way to Vienna, we stopped off for a few hours in Salzburg, a city famous for its music. We visited locations that had served as settings for the movie *The Sound Of Music*. We also visited the house where Mozart had lived two hundred years before, and watched a film about his life. It is a pity that he died so young, at the age of thirty-two.

On the morning of the twenty-sixth, we caught a train bound for Venice, Italy. This is a city of watery beauty, wide canals, and special barges called gondolas. The water level in this area is very high and foundations are weak. The first and second storey of buildings are usually inundated with water and useless. Even beautiful St Mark's Church had to be propped up because it is situated at a low level.

We journeyed on to Milan and visited St Bartholomew Cathedral. The inside of the church is very glamorous. Since it is of Gothic style, I found it to be especially expansive. We also visited a palace in Florence where many famous works of art were on display. The statue of young David brimmed with energy, as if it were alive. The strong muscles emanated brute strength. A pebble taken from David's pocket and pitched from his sling hit the forehead of the Philistine and killed him. This statue lured many tourists there.

After our tour of Florence, we arrived safely back in Geneva. On February 3, Rita and I were guests at the home of Melitta Budiner, a colleague of Rita. Next morning, we set off for the snow mountains in Vallee. We journeyed by train from Geneva to Sierre/Sion. There, we transferred to a special mountain train destined for Montana Crans (3,000 meters above sea level). Upon our arrival, we hurried off to watch a curling game. The players seemed to enjoy their game very much. Later, we attended an air show and watched the planes soar above the snow-capped mountains. It was a thoroughly enjoyable day. I had never before experienced the pleasures of life on a snowy plateau, and I therefore found it very exhilarating.

We travelled on to Amsterdam in Holland and visited a clogs factory. They made clogs galore for tourists to purchase as souvenirs. The parable of the prodigal son was depicted on one pair. Another pair was painted with colourful pictures and were beautiful enough to wear to a wedding banquet. Yet another pair was made especially for going to church.

We were happy to savour authentic Dutch fishing village fare at lunch. All workers serving the tourists were dressed in traditional festive garb of vivid colours and styles. The food was tasty and aromatic. The fishing villages had their own special charm and were preferred by tourists.

Holland's dairy products are world famous. I found it most interesting to visit a cheese factory, which also produced goat's cheese. Each hunk was around two or three pounds in weight. There were many kinds of cheese made from cow's milk. These varied in size from small slices of one to three pounds to enormous pieces of twenty to thirty pounds.

On the broad plains of Holland's countryside, one could stroll up to huge and ancient windmills. As we were leaving La Hague in the Peace Palace, we met an amiable Indonesian couple who treated us to afternoon tea at the Parliament Buildings.

## 34. Revisiting England

From the Hook of Holland, we travelled by ferry to Harwick, a harbour in southern England, and then journeyed to London's Liverpool Street by train. The Rev. Bennett came to meet us and took us to her home in the Great Missenden.

I attended, by invitation, the Synod of the Diocese of Canterbury and York on February 15, 1985. The chairman welcomed me and presented me with the Book of Alternative Services, published in 1980.

During a break at the Synod, Archbishop Runcie came up to the second floor where I was sitting to shake hands and give me a welcoming kiss. I was surprised to meet Archdeacon and Mrs. Ian Harland again. They had been on the pilgrimage tour and I was glad to know that Archdeacon Harland had been consecrated bishop. Among those invited to attend as honoured guests were the Right Rev. Richard Rutt, who was Bishop of Taejon Diocese, South Korea. After the conference, Miss Rachel Vincy, publicity manager of Darton, Longman & Todd, took Rita and I to the Victoria Restaurant for lunch, and we discussed the publication of the book *Much Beloved Daughter*.

On the seventeenth, I attended the English service at St Martin's and met with Mr. Ted Harrison after Eucharist. I raised two issues with him. I wanted to have the original manuscript for the book after publication, and, if I should suddenly die, I wanted the royalties from *Much Beloved Daughter* to be donated to the Movement for the Ordination of Women. Mr. Harrison accepted both my requests.

That day, I responded to the request of the Anglican Church Women of St Martin's and gave a short talk on my pilgrimage to Jerusalem. It was important to me to convey that the pilgrimage had not been merely a tour to see the attractions, but that it had deepened my appreciation of Jesus as Saviour. Even though "seeing is believing," memories fade. To believe in Christ, we must live in Christ. St Paul asserted, "To live is Christ." Faith and action must complement each other.

I visited England's famous universities, Oxford and Cambridge, cultural centres and university towns. I visited Cambridge on February 19 and Oxford on the twentieth. Cambridge University's King's College Chapel, dedicated to St Mary and St Nicholas, is a Gothic-style building. I found its ceiling to be very beautiful. Oxford's Christ Church has a

Norman-style domed top, and is a building of great historical value. These two universities have made unparalleled contributions to the world of culture over the last two to three centuries. Even though I did not study at either school, I have been more or less affected by their cultures, as I was born in the British colony of Hong Kong.

On March 5, I was a guest at a cocktail party given by Dean and Mrs. Webster, held in the church hall of St Paul's Cathedral. Dean Webster introduced me to everyone, and I gave a short speech: "I thank the hosts for organizing this event, where I can meet with this elite society of writers, poets, and professors. I left China three years ago and am in England for the second time. My sister Rita is with me. After my immigration to Canada, God blessed me by allowing me to be an honorary assistant at St Matthew's and St John's Church, and my colleagues and I serve in co-operation and harmony.

"No one has ever slighted me because I was a woman priest. I have passed through countless raging tempests, through thirty years of political movement in China, and God's hand is always there to hold me up, to conquer the darkness and rampage. God lives in human hearts and He was with me every moment. Even though I was misunderstood by many in China, I have learned to follow Jesus' teaching: 'Forgive them, for they do not know what they do.' Moreover, a forgiving heart can attain spiritual freedom, and joy will pour in."

# Part Four
# 1985–1992

✤ ✤ ✤

## 35. Moving to a New Home

The pilgrimage and tour of Europe and England concluded on March 14, 1985. When I returned to Toronto, the church was lively and progressing, and I made a change in my living arrangements. As I was elderly, my sister Rita resolved to forsake over thirty years of comfortable and serene living in Geneva and emigrate to Canada so that we might spend our remaining years together. Her sense of kinship and her love were beyond compare.

On April 27, 1985, we moved into Rita's new apartment at 2330 Bridletowne Circle in Scarborough, Ontario. Our niece Sze-Sze, my brother Ching-Yiu's daughter, had planned to live with us, but it proved to be too far a commute to the University of Toronto where she was studying. Instead, she rented a room in the city and came home to stay for weekends and holidays.

## 36. Joining the Activities of Toronto Churches

On March 12, 1986, I was invited to speak to the ladies' fellowship of All Soul's Church, and I shared the experiences of my life and my work with them. They were delighted to be in the amiable fellowship of a Christian woman who could offer a Chinese perspective.

On the sixteenth, the Anglican Consultative Council Primate's Meeting was held at St Paul's Church. Twenty-eight archbishops attended an evensong, which started at 4 p.m. Archbishop Runcie preached. At tea afterwards, I met Archbishop Scott, Dr. Runcie, Bishop K. H. Ting of China, Bishop Luke Choa, bishops from Japan and Korea, and Archdeacon Yong Ping-Chung of Sabah.

On the eighteenth, Chinese and Western friends held a farewell dinner for Bishop Ting at Sai-Woo Restaurant. Consul General Hsia

Jung-Tseng was concerned about whether I was receiving my pension from China, and Bishop Ting promised to look into it upon his return to China.

On Palm Sunday, Bishop Kwong of Hong Kong visited our church and preached. His sermon was based on "the difference between people and animals is that people have souls." A reception was held for Bishop Kwong at Lucky Years Restaurant.

All Saints' Chinese Church was consecrated by Archbishop Lewis Garnsworthy. Also in attendance were Bishop Arthur Brown and Bishop Parke-Taylor. A banquet of twenty tables was held at the Pacific Restaurant. The incumbent, the Rev. Kenneth Fung, was diligent in spreading the gospel. For this event, I sent the following greeting: "The Church stands in glory for the Kingdom of Heaven / A banquet is prepared for spiritual nourishment."

## 37. 1986 Canterbury Pilgrimage and Joining Hands Conference

I attended the Canterbury Pilgrimage and Joining Hands Conference, held on April 14-27, 1986. Thousands of women from all over the Anglican Communion came to Canterbury to discuss the importance of women in ministry and to fight for their right to serve the church throughout the world. Representatives came from Ghana, Uganda, Hong Kong, Brazil, India, the United States, Canada, and Australia.

On the eighteenth, the first wave of pilgrims arrived and were greeted by the enthusiastic welcome of a large crowd of male and female priests. In the pitch-dark basement of Canterbury Cathedral, an all-night vigil was held. I was invited to light the first candle. Even though another woman escorted me, I caught my foot on a protruding slab on the floor as soon as I started walking, and I fell. Luckily, I was not hurt, and I quickly got up. Everyone in the church had feared otherwise, but with thanks to God, I had peace that surpassed understanding. All over the church, small candles were lighted. Those tiny flames drove away the darkness, and the way became clear. That night, the pilgrimage visited Thomas A. Becket's tomb to pay respect. Archbishop Becket (1117-1170) had been murdered for his opposition to King Henry ii.

On Saturday, April 19, a Eucharist was held in the sanctuary of Canterbury Cathedral. I felt honoured to be in the offertory procession.

Sixteen bishops, a hundred priests, one hundred and seventy-five deaconesses, and a congregation of over two thousand were in attendance for the service. Mrs. Mary Tanner was invited to preach. Her theme was, "God chose us; we did not choose God." Every word of her sermon moved our hearts and incited us to be more ardent in our ministry to spread the gospel. Thirteen languages were used in passing the Peace.

On Wednesday, the twenty-third, Miss Veronica drove the Rev. Joyce Bennett, the Rev. Mary Au, and me to a visit with Miss E. Atkins, the former principal of St. Stephen's Girls' College of Hong Kong. As Bishop Gilbert Baker was ill in hospital, I visited him on the afternoon of the twenty-fifth. On Tuesday, the twenty-ninth, the sun was shining, and we visited Guildford Cathedral where Bishop Baker had once been a suffragan bishop.

## 38. In Memory of the Late Bishop Gilbert Baker

After my business in England was over, I flew back to Toronto on Wednesday, April 30. My brother Hon-Yiu and my sister-in-law came to meet me. Awaiting me at home was the news that Bishop Baker of Hong Kong had passed away on April 29.

On the evening of July 2, I was inspired to write a few words in memory of Bishop Baker:

> With his body resting among blossoms,
> His spirit is running towards God's Kingdom.
> Following the precedence of Bishop Hall,
> Women priests he ordained two more.
> America and the Third World had his treks,
> Back to England with no regrets.
> Equality and human rights he raised,
> may his accomplishments be praised.

## 39. The Tenth Anniversary Celebration of Ordination of Women to Priesthood in the ACC

In celebration of the tenth anniversary of ordination of women to priesthood in the Anglican Church of Canada, a conference for women priests was held in Bolton from November 22 to November 25, 1986. I am grateful to St John's Chinese Congregation, the incumbent Rev. Edmund Der, and the advisory board members for their financial and spiritual support that allowed me to be part of this event.

The theme of the conference was "Journey into Wholeness," meaning our spiritual progress must be like water in a river, endlessly flowing forth. The highest spiritual leader in the Anglican Church of Canada, Archbishop Michael Peers, joined us there. His gregarious personality brought much warmth and friendliness to the gathering. He strongly urged us to furtherance as living witnesses to Christ and thoroughly analyzed the biblical evidence that the ordination of women priests concurred with Christ's teachings. Lord Jesus had always honoured women. God created men and women according to His own image, and gave them sacred tasks in order to continually bring about a more ideal and more beautiful world.

I was the only Chinese woman priest at the conference. The others in attendance were all Canadian women priests or women lay leaders. A total of forty-five people attended, from every province. The nature of their work varied. Some were incumbents of parishes, school or hospital chaplains, seminary professors, social workers, and so on. One was in reclusion. Some were responsible for several parishes, as many as six. In every corner of the earth, whether plains or hills, country or cities, there were the beautiful feet of those who bring good news.

Women have the responsibility of being messengers of Christianity and social development, and they constitute a rich human resource. They can truly hold up "half the earth." These women can be single, married, grandmothers, sharing ministry with their husbands, or priests with happy families. Democracy and freedom has been fully realized inside the church, and its superior social system shines.

That anniversary celebration had two special features. First, there were observers present. The Anglican Church had sent a male priest to join in all our activities. He was the only "blossom among many green leaves." Another observer was a female social worker sent by the Roman Catholic Church. These two handled all the communications and reporting of events of the celebration. By doing this, the Anglican Church indicated the importance it placed on the conference.

Second, the spouse of a priest from the Anglican Diocese of Vancouver, who possessed a profound knowledge of music, was invited to join the conference as music director. She coordinated sacred music for all the worship services and programs and made them all the more fascinating.

Other than hymns of praise, we used art and simple rhythms and dances to express our moods of worship. Three consecutive days of heart-to-heart chats and three Eucharist services made the conference lively and interesting. As there were no theme talks, and the music was stimulating, we were all moved to open up and share our innermost selves and experiences in ministry for our mutual spiritual benefit. That colourful and lively atmosphere penetrated deeply into my soul and left a profound impression. We all agreed: "This is a new pattern. It is not dry at all."

During these celebrations, I raised my eyes to see an army of women priests, bright and spirited, steadfast and courageous. In resolute steps, they marched from tradition to break new ground and fortify their numbers. How could I not proffer my sincere reverent heart to thank God for His enormous benedictions!

May the number of men and women serving the true God in Trinity grow and be fortified day by day. May their power to move people be multiplied, their light shine forth before all people. May God be glorified!

On November 30, a Thanksgiving Eucharist was held in Toronto's St Michael and All Angels' Church, concluding the celebration.

## 40. My Trip to China

From March 26 to April 27, 1987, the Rev. Dr. Robert Browne, communications consultant of the Archbishop of Canterbury and a member of the Anglican Consultative Council, led American cameraman Grant Mitchell, my sister Rita, and me on a trip to China. The purpose of the trip was to produce a video tape of my visits to the Three-Self Movement Church of China and the different parishes of Chunghua Shungkunghui where I had served. The tape would provide discussion material for the 1988 Lambeth Conference. The entire trip took thirty-three days. Of these, twenty-six were spent in China, one in Macau, and the remainder in Hong Kong.

We visited many places in China, including Shanghai, Nanjing, Beijing, Tienjien, Sian, Guilin, Guangzhou, Shaoqing, Beihai, and Hepu.

I had travelled to many parts of China before I left for Canada. During this visit, I noticed that both the small towns and the cities had improved in appearance. Jinling Hotel of Nanjing is in the centre of town. From its revolving restaurant, the entire Nanjing could be seen. In Beijing, skyscrapers had replaced the walled-in family homesteads of old. The luxury of the Lido Hotel in Beijing surpassed certain other large hotels in Europe and North America. Staying in such a splendid and modern hotel, with the most up-to-date facilities and management, made me feel like a traveller abroad. Visitors, having caught the China fever, came from all over the world. If prospective guests had not made reservations six months in advance, they were turned away. The demand for English-speaking tour guides exceeded the supply. Tourism had developed at an amazing pace.

In all the places I visited, I deeply appreciated the improvement in people's standard of living. Everyone was better dressed. Street sanitation had improved. Many highways had been built leading straight to Beijing, and the road surfaces had been paved to reduce dust.

During earlier times in Shaoqing, Chunghua Shungkunghui had established a parish church, a school, and women's literacy classes on Hay Wall Lane. Deaconess Lucy Vincent of Britain had been a minister here. Other male and female missionaries had been sent here by the Church of England to spread the gospel. Suffragan Bishop MoYung Yin of the Guangdong Diocese of Chunghua Shungkunghui received his education and learned about religion during his youth here in the Chunghua Shungkunghui Church of Shaoqin.

I was ordained a priest in the Chunghua Shungkunghui Church of Shaoqin. The wooden church had become dilapidated, and was torn down soon after the Liberation. A new two-storey building had been erected on the extensive landscape. The ground floor served as a church, and on the second floor were dormitories with rather good facilities. This new building was named "Comfort House," and it was open to retired clergy for vacations. The Seven Stars Lake was within walking distance, and the Guangzhou Christian Youth Fellowship and clergy groups held many retreats at this pleasant site.

The first parish I visited in Shanghai was the Shanghai Community Church. The Rev. Shen Yi-Fan (later consecrated bishop) was rector. He was filled with the power of the Spirit, and with the cooperative assistance of the Revs. Pang Shing-Yung, Yang An-Ting, and Pang En-Mei (female), the worship atmosphere was very rich. The huge church choir sang resounding praises to God and enhanced the joyful sense of His presence in the congregation. I delivered greetings from the Chinese parishes in Toronto, Canada, and gave a short talk in Cantonese. I was elated to experience complete religious freedom!

The Jinling Union Theological College in Nanjing was the highest educational institute for Christian theology in the nation. Classes in the college had been restored in 1981 and many ardent church ministers of the next generation were trained here. Its graduates were sent to churches in large cities, such as Beijing, Shanghai, Tienjin, and even Sian, Guangzhou, and Beihai. These new forces were responsible for advancing the Three-Self Movement.

Mr. Chang Ching-Lung had returned to China from his studies in Canada. His contributions to the college and his influence on the students were great. Bishop Principal Ting gave his best for his students and achieved distinguished results.

Incidently, Bishop Ting, who was also Chairman of the Three-Self Movement Committee, was in Beijing for the People's congress while we were there. He took time out of his busy schedule to treat us to dinner at Tsui Ya Restaurant. Other guests included the Rev. Yin Ji-Tseng of Beijing and the Rev. Kan Shieh-Ching. We were excited when we heard from Bishop Ting that the economy of my Motherland was booming and the work of the Three-Self Movement was developing very rapidly. We chatted freely and extensively, and I really enjoyed our gathering.

After dinner, Bishop Ting handed me an envelope and bade me not to open until I was back in my hotel room. When I opened it, I found one thousand renminbi in foreign exchange coupons. It was an exceedingly generous gift. After thinking about it, I realized that when Bishop Ting had been in Toronto, Consul General Shia Chung Jeng had inquired about my pension. Because of this, Bishop Ting had given this huge sum to me in person while I was in China. Bishop Ting was fair and prudent in managing the affairs of the Three-Self Movement.

Besides the national Jinling Union Theological College, there were other local seminaries, such as Huabei (North China), Huatung (East China), Huanan (South China), and Guangdong Theological Colleges. They had sprung up like bamboo shoots after spring rain. Moreover, in order to promote church revival, volunteer study classes of three to six months duration were held. This situation was similar to what the prophet Ezekiel saw in the "valley of dry bones" when he prophesied, "I will make breath enter you and you will come to life" (Ezek. 37:5). Christians, together with the Three-Self Movement, had attained indelible results. Everywhere we visited, fellow church workers and Christians showed us ardent hospitality.

We took advantage of the opportunity to fly to the northwest region of China Shansi to visit the Rev. Tien Jing-Foo in Sian. The Rev. Tien had accompanied Bishop Ting and Lin Tschuen on a visit to India.

When we visited, the Rev. Tien told us that three churches had been revived in Shian. On average, Sunday worship attendance was at eight hundred. In other words, over two thousand people attended church services every Sunday. There were weekly Bible study groups, attended by over four hundred people each week. The zeal for the word in parishioners was truly commendable. Unfortunately, we could not visit for long. Yet, as the Rev. Dr. Brown said in his prayer during worship, "The great love of God holds us together despite the physical distance between us. The time for us to love each other is short, but our fellowship is dear."

The Church of Our Saviour in Guangzhou celebrated its second anniversary (after revival) on April 12 with a thanksgiving service. By invitation from the rector, the Rev. Li Tak-Fei, I delivered the sermon to a congregation that filled the pews. After the service, the Rev. Li and the advisory board members hosted a luncheon at Boon Kai (Riverside) Restaurant to welcome us. That evening, Christian brothers and sisters of The Church of Our Saviour threw a banquet reception for us at Guanhzhou Restaurant. They talked excitedly about the church's revival. Before China's Liberation, this had been an Anglican cathedral. Now, denominations no longer existed, and all were united into the Three-Self Church.

There was an exciting piece of news: Bishop Kwong-Kit of the Diocese of Hong Kong and Macau had donated an electronic organ to the parish. The Rev. David Leigh personally installed it and then led in a performance of sacred music. Afterwards, the Rev. Wang Wei-Fan, a professor from the Jinling Union Theological College, held evangelistic services on five consecutive nights. There were no empty seats at those services.

We travelled from Guangzhou to the Seven Stars Cavern at Shaoqin. The picturesque lakes and mountains mesmerized us all. The Shaoqin Christian Church had been revived in 1986 and was now located on Cheng Chung Road, next to the Shaoqin Theatre. The parishioners of the church had received news of our visit from Guangzhou, and they had gathered at the church early in the morning in order to welcome us. Unfortunately, as we had been late leaving Guangzhou, we did not arrive there until late afternoon. I felt sorry to have kept them waiting. We sang many hymns at that gathering, of which the "Ode to Joy" was a full expression of our sentiments. We also interceded for each other and offered praise and thanksgiving. The rector, the Rev. Yeung Hung-Tao, was in the hospital because of an eye ailment, so we visited him there.

On the day before we left Shaoqin, we toured the city and searched out Watershed Mountain Range—a mountain near Hsinxing—in order to tape some video footage of the area. I had travelled through there in January 1944 on my way to Shaoqin for my ordination ceremony.

We then hurried on to Beihai in order to celebrate Easter, and arrived at the Beihai Hotel on the eve of Easter. The Rev. Cheung Yat-Sun came to visit us, and later on, Dr. Lam Yee-Yin and his wife Dr. Lam Yan of Po Yan Hospital (now called the People's Hospital) also came for a joyful gathering.

The Rev. Cheung Yat-Sun was officiant at the Easter service. The Rev. Chan Tai-Wai preached, and I celebrated Eucharist with the eucharistic rite published by the Three-Self Movement, which had just arrived by air from Nanjing. Parishioners filled the church to capacity, and the atmosphere was very enthusiastic.

After enjoying a lunch reception given by the Beihai parishioners, we pressed on to Hepu and reached the church by that afternoon. A large crowd awaited us, and large red posters of welcome had been hung on each side of the door. From the throng emerged two lovely little girls, who reverently presented a bunch of pink roses to Dr. Brown and me. As soon as we set foot on the church steps, welcoming firecrackers were set off that rocked all of Hepu. Inside the church were posters bearing both English and Chinese words of welcome for Dr. Brown, me, and all who were guests. More than twenty Christian friends came to the gathering from the neighbouring counties of Gaodeh, Changlo, Gungguan.

Of my visit to Hepu, I was fascinated by the tour we had of the People's Hospital. Director Dr. Lam Yee-Yin explained that the hospital had been established in 1886 by the Missionary Society of England but was taken over by the government in 1952. In 1947, there had been only two doctors—Director Lam and his wife. Since 1952, the number of medical staff had increased rapidly. At the time of my visit, there were over five hundred: 83 resident interns, 31 staff specialists and 129 nurses.

Before China's Liberation, a limited supply of medicine had come from Britain, but services had expanded. For instance, in the fifties, outpatients numbered a hundred a day. Now there were two hundred. Hospital beds had increased from one hundred to four hundred. The death rate of the nine to ten thousand patients who stayed in the hospital each year had been reduced to only 1.6 percent. Besides internal medicine, other specialties, such as general surgery, neurology, cardiology, urology, orthopaedics, and neuro-oncology, were available. The People's

Hospital had become the teaching hospital of Guangshi Province, where medical interns from Janjiang Medical School and Guangshi Medical School were trained. The populace called it the "Advanced Hospital" or the "Progressive Hospital." This wonderful progress was a result of government support, which enabled the massive recruitment of medical workers.

After visiting Hepu, we completed our visit to China and its churches, and arrived in Hong Kong on April 22. We stayed at the New World Hotel in Kowloon, and went out to visit St John's Cathedral, St Paul's Church and All Saints' Church. On April 23, we visited my birthplace, Aberdeen, and ate lunch at the Jumbo Floating Restaurant while enjoying the seascape. Bishop Kwong gave us a reception that evening at the Yuet Kong Spring Restaurant.

The next day, we took a hydrofoil to Macau to visit St Mark's Church. When peace was restored after the Second World War, we Christians had left the rented Robert Morrison chapel for our own premises on Pedro Nolasco da Silva, and St Mark's was borne from our love and toil. Now St Mark's had established Choi Ko Secondary School and ran it with great success. The rector of St. Mark's was the Rev. Leung Wing-Hong, who nurtured young minds with a balanced program of both general and religious education. Parishioners planted their faith on a firm foundation and led active spiritual lives.

I had been away from Macau for almost half a century, and I found it totally transformed. East Asia University was a newly established educational institute that effectively upgraded the younger generation. Its modern design was comparable to those in Hong Kong. The sanitation of the streets was in marked contrast to that of the forties—like heaven and hell.

After our day-long excursion to Macau, my relatives (the Li clan) held a banquet at Dunhuang Restaurant on Nathan Road, Kowloon, to thank Dr. Brown and Mr. Mitchell for their help in completing the video recording of my life and work in China. We talked about the abundant harvest of experiences we had garnered from our visit to China, and our relatives shared in our happiness. Dr. Brown and Mr. Mitchell then flew to Singapore for a meeting the next day.

On the evening of April 25, my niece Li Sze-Kit (Mrs. Lai Chak-Luen) invited me to her home on Victoria Peak for supper. As I looked down though the dark at the Hong Kong harbour, I saw ocean liners from all over the world shimmer as they streamed quietly through the waters, enchanting and glamorous. No wonder Hong Kong is called the Pearl of the Orient.

## 41. A Happy Birthday and Receiving My Degree

*My Birthday Celebration*

Other than my visit to China, two events stand out from 1987: my eightieth birthday and receiving my honorary Doctorate of Divinity degree.

I celebrated my eightieth birthday on May 5. I vividly recall how the Rev. Edmund Der and the parishioners of St Matthew's and St John's celebrated the occasion with a thanksgiving service. The Rev. Kenneth Fung and his flock from All Saints' Chinese Church, the Rev. Tsang Wing-Fai, and the Rev. Tsui Pui-Ho were invited to join in our celebration. Archbishop Lewis Garnsworthy of Toronto gave me a lot of encouragement in his sermon. The newly renovated church hall was renamed "Li Tim-Oi Hall." The young people of the parish entertained the congregation with a short skit based on the story of my life. Over two hundred people, including several municipal aldermen and members of the provincial parliament, attended the banquet. Premier Peterson sent a special greeting that was read aloud during the banquet and filled me with excitement.

The youth fellowships, other members of the congregation, St Matthew's congregation, and my colleagues presented me with commemorative gifts. St John's Voice No. 9 contained a collection of articles honouring my birthday celebration. The hymn "Praise To God, For Years Of Grace" from *Hymns of Universal Praise* was printed on the first page to accentuate the importance of the occasion. I was overwhelmed and abashed as I spoke:

"Because you love the Lord, you spread your love onto me and bestowed me with immeasurable cheers. I examined myself and found no special talents, only a little faith not worthy of mention. The true God in Trinity enwrapped me with His love, which was wide and long and high and deep, so I could spend the evening of my life happily overseas. Will I be able to witness for the gospel with my remaining years as I wish? No one can know. Let us pray for each other, please. The years of worshipping together have filled my heart with glory.

"During the long years of my life, I have fulfilled two great wishes. Firstly, I hoped to go abroad to visit relatives and travel, and this wish was fulfilled. Moreover, I was even able to stay in Toronto. Secondly, I hoped to go back and visit the different churches. My trip has been safe and happy, for God's blessings have always been with me. Now I am going to face a challenge. My health is weak, and I am going for an operation on my nose. May God protect me so I may recover after a short rest, so I may again take up what work of the church I can still bear. In my mind is the second verse from 'The King Of Love My Shepherd Is': 'Where streams of living waters flow / my ransomed soul He leadeth / And where the verdant pastures grow / With food celestial feedeth.' This is my sincere wish. May God bless all those who are here."

## *Receiving a Doctorate of Divinity Degree*

I received my honorary Doctorate of Divinity degree from the General Theological Seminary in New York, which has a 170-year history. Rita accompanied me on my trip to New York to receive it. We arrived in New York on May 18, and were fortunate to have Mr. Chung Yung-Hong, a student of Columbia University, meet us at the airport and take us to the guest wing of the seminary. We had some free time in the evening, so after a Chinese meal, Mr. Chung drove us around the bustling and glamorous city. The lights were especially delightful.

On the evening of the 19th, the principal of the General Theological Seminary, James C. Fenhagen, gave a reception for the five candidates who were to receive honorary degrees (two women and three men), their relatives, and other New York dignitaries.

On May 20, the ceremony to confer the doctorate degrees was held at the seminary's convocation hall. The hall had been decorated to solemn effect for the distinguished guests. Majestic music was played that reverberated in my heart and filled me with awe and joy. Whenever a doctorate degree was conferred, the audience broke out in applause. When it was my turn, the applause was louder than ever and lasted for several minutes. At that moment, the joy in my heart was indescribable. I kept on repeating praises and thanksgiving to the Lord. I met some old friends on this special occasion and also made some new ones. Several senior seminary students were interested in my experiences during the many years of my ministry.

## 42. A Special Guest of the Lambeth Conference

My most memorable experience of 1988 was attending the Lambeth Conference as a special guest. The Lambeth Conference was held in Canterbury in southern England, a two-hour drive from London. Canterbury was the sacred site upon which Christianity first reached England from the European continent. It was also a pilgrimage centre during the Middle Ages.

Thanks to the material and spiritual support of St John's Chinese Congregation in Toronto, I was able to accept the invitation to attend. It was by God's bounteous goodness, and I felt honoured. Moreover, thanks to Bishop Arthur Brown's assistance, the diocese made it possible for Rita to accompany me so I could have the best of care on my trip. The Conference executives sent us two tickets just in time for me and my sister to be admitted into Canterbury Cathedral. Unfortunately, there were not enough seats and many had to be turned away.

The event began on July 17, with a stately and solemn eucharistic service. Before the service, 525 bishops robed in purple, the chairman and executive secretary of the Anglican Consultative Council, church leaders from all over the world, and numerous special guests gathered in front of the cathedral doors. Then, in unison, they marched inside for the opening ceremony. Almost two hundred bishops' wives were also present. This particular Lambeth Conference made history by allowing women clergy to attend.

Archbishop Runcie delivered his opening speech, and he said, "We come from afar to the Twelfth Lambeth Conference in order to be together, to share, learn, listen, and seek the word of God so we may be encouraged and strengthened in our leadership to further develop the church. I hope that God will use us, and through us may His wonderful will to build a better future be realized."

On the eve of the Lambeth Conference, Archbishop Runcie conferred three honourary Doctorates of Theology at Kent University to Bishop K. H. Ting of the Three-Self Church of China, Cardinal Romero of Central America, and Archbishop Michael Peers of Canada. This splendid event made the Lambeth Conference even more colourful.

I was to meet with Archbishop Runcie and Bishop Ting on the evening of July 20. The video tape of my work in China, *Return to Hepu*, was shown to over two hundred people in two sittings in the Kent University theatre. After the first sitting, Canon Christopher Hall spoke in support of the ordination of woman priests, and Bishop Ting revealed that half of the students of the Union Theological College in Nanjing were female.

## *In Support of the Ordination of Women to Priesthood*

On the morning of July 31, the bishops and their wives attending the Lambeth Conference held a Eucharist at St Paul's Cathedral in London. Many of us hurried to London from Canterbury to join a March Past, scheduled to take place when the service was over. We flew high flags, coloured balloons, and banners and formed a massive army of smart-looking peaceful demonstrators in support of the ordination of woman to priesthood in Britain. Both the male and female members of the city police assisted the March Past. When the bishops came out from the Cathedral, many cheerfully showed their ardent support.

The most significant discussion of the 1988 Lambeth Conference concerned the ordination of women priests and the consecration of women bishops. The outcome of the discussion was favourable: the ordination of women to priesthood in Britain would be put into practice by 1993.

Archbishop Michael Peers of Canada spoke out strongly in his support of the ordination of women priests. In his opinion, women priests truly strengthened the clergy body.

On the clear and silent night of July 31, the sky above Kent University was set alight by fireworks. These were made possible by the Bishop of Ottawa and added festivity to the conference.

## *In Conclusion*

Let me say that it is only proper for us, not to discriminate between sexes, but with one heart and one mind bear witness to Christ. "For all of you who were baptized into Christ have clothed yourselves with Christ. There is neither Jew nor Greek, slave nor free, male nor female, for you are all one in Christ Jesus" (Gal.3:27,28). If we stand steadfast in our faith, and both male and female cooperate in bringing heaven on earth, decisive victory is certain through the power of the Holy Spirit. Besides, is not our God an omnipotent God and our help in ages past? "For no one can lay any foundation other than the one already laid, which is Jesus Christ" (I Cor. 3:11).

## 43. The Consecration of the Rev. Barbara Harris

By the blessing of God, I was invited to attend the consecration of the first woman bishop of the Episcopal Church of the United States as a special guest of Presiding Bishop Edmund Browning. The consecration service took place in Boston on February 11, 1989. So once again I joined the queue of clergy streaming into this unforgettable, magnificent assembly.

For two thousand years, church ministry has been fulfilled by men. This has helped to form the erroneous conception that only men could be ordained as priests. Women have had to be content with the level of deaconess, with no possibility of further advancement. The Rev. Barbara Harris's election to bishopric broke through the barrier of tradition and can be viewed as a ground-breaking act of innovation in the church. Under the guidance of the Holy Spirit, the church caught up with the times and entered into a new era. God's goodness and mercy shone forth on this wonderful occasion of the consecration of a woman bishop.

As no Episcopal church in Boston was large enough to seat the huge crowd of 8,500 expected to attend the consecration ceremony, it was held at Hynes Convention Centre. With proper decorations, the premise was solemn and dignified. Inside, an organ and a brass band supported the majestic voices of St Paul's Cathedral choir, the choir of the Chinese congregation, and other choirs in glorifying God. The attendees echoed with joyful praises. These filled the Centre and touched the heart of everyone. Even though the ceremony lasted for three hours, the congregation's interest and excitement did not wane.

Over fifty bishops surrounded the Rev. Harris to lay hands on her head. She later said, "At that moment, I realized the authority of the Apostles passing on." The Rev. Harris was the seventeenth black to be consecrated as bishop in the U.S. Episcopal Church. Bishop David Johnson of St Paul's Cathedral said, "Today is a historic day of joy and real celebration. It is God's will that Bishop Harris has been elected bishop. It demonstrates that God is Father and also Mother."

The Lord Jesus chose Barbara Harris to be the first woman bishop. I was delighted and thankful. Lord Jesus said, "You did not choose me, but I chose you and appointed you to go and bear fruit—fruit that will last" (John 15:16).

## 44. A Pacific Cruise

My sister Rita and I took a cruise vacation, a novel experience for me. We sailed on the modern 62,000-ton *Star Princess* with fifteen hundred passengers from all over the world. We were literally "all in the same boat"; our aim of meaningful first-class enjoyment united us. There were over seven hundred hard-working and courteous crew members. What a busy ship!

Although a ship, it resembled the epitome of a modern urban centre. The fourteen clean and bright decks were connected by elevators. Among its facilities were recreation rooms, shops, photo studios, beauty salons, casinos, and exercise gyms. The open deck for sun-bathing was on the fourteenth level. One could swim in the heated pool or lounge on the neat rows of deck chairs, resting and savouring the fresh ocean breeze. How enjoyable!

The ocean remained calm. Even seniors who used walking canes and wheelchairs could go steadily about. We sailed northwards along the coast from Vancouver to Alaska. From the star side, one could view the scenery along the coast, the distant, pristine, snow-capped mountain ranges and the bizarre and outlandish rock formations along the shore. From the port side, stretching between the blue sky and the aqua sea, was the endless horizon. The majesty of the Pacific Ocean filled our eyes. Touched by the endless sea and the infinite sky, passengers strolling on deck left behind the vain and busy throng of urban life and lifted their hearts in adoration for the Creator. Their pursuit of the natural world led them to worship the supernatural God, the omnipotent Creator of nature, full of power and glory.

Religious activities took place on the fifth deck, and there was a cruise chaplain to look after the flock on board. Mass was held every morning at 7 a.m, and Sunday worship was held at 5 p.m. The worship program was international and non-denominational. It included silent prayer, litany, intercession, hymn-singing, sermon, and benediction. It was a pity that only around a hundred people attended the service. This fact indicated that very few people worshipped God or had their minds on heavenly things. Brothers and Sisters in Christ, have you and I ever considered responding to God's great call to spread the gospel to this generation?

## 45. Reflections during Convalescence

On December 30, 1990, at dawn of the last Sunday of the year, I seriously injured my spine in an accidental fall at home. Thanks to the assistance of Dr. Arnold Wong, I was taken to Grace Hospital for an X-ray. This revealed a compression fracture of a lumbar spine vertebrae. Since the fractured fragments were compressed on the spinal cord and its network of nerves, the resulting pain was as brutal as having a dagger thrust into the bone. The agony was indescribable. For three months, I had to lie still in bed. I could not even feed myself. Mrs. Pandora Yeung was kind and patient, for she was always there to feed me, mouthful after mouthful, at supper time. Her love was truly remarkable, unparalleled and commendable.

From late February to the end of July, I was in and out of three different hospitals for treatment. At the beginning of July, my condition was a little better, and the hospital staff patiently trained me, step by step, to get up, sit up, feed myself, and use a walker. Towards the end of July, I was sent to Mount Sinai Hospital for three weeks of physiotherapy so that my limbs could recover their movements to a certain degree. At last, on July 31, and in compliance with the hospital's astute arrangement, I was sent home to convalesce. According to the doctors, a spinal injury suffered by an elderly person took a longer time to heal. Moreover, my recovery would never be 100 percent. What could I do? Only forbear in patience.

Under the leadership of the Rev. Edmund Der, who was full of Christian love, parishioners prayed devoutly for my early recovery. By the mercy and blessing of God, the prayers of the righteous were answered. Parishioners, young, old, and middle-aged, came to my hospital bed and my home to visit and comfort me in various entertaining ways, and I experienced Christian fellowship to its fullest. They brought with them generous amounts of nourishing soups, nutritious snacks, fruits, and flowers. I received cards, letters, phone calls, and a myriad of other material and spiritual support. I was deeply grateful to receive such immeasurable love and friendship, but regretted that I could do nothing to reciprocate it or express my gratitude. I could only wish that the blessing of Proverbs 11:25 be upon all of them: "A generous man will prosper; he who refreshes others will himself be refreshed." Jesus said, "I tell you the truth, whatever you did for one of the least of these brothers of mine, you did for me" (Matt. 25:40).

The care and concern I received during my convalescence opened my spiritual eyes. I deeply appreciated that my Christian brothers and sisters did not merely listen to the word; they did what it said. St James taught us that faith must be accompanied by deeds. Faith is made complete by deeds. The spiritual progress my brothers and sisters were making was pleasing to God. It was applaudable and worthy of celebration.

## *The Power of Faith*

"And without faith it is impossible to please God, because anyone who comes to him must believe that he exists and that he rewards those who earnestly seek him" (Heb. 11:6). It is possible for those with stalwart faith to overcome afflictions, for faith is victory. Human nature has its frailty, and when I was in pain, I could not help but feel troubled. Questions swirled in my mind: Does God understand my torment? When will my suffering end? Do I have the strength to overcome my afflictions? What is the proper attitude towards suffering?

My troubled thoughts were swept away by the following resolves: God is the ever-living God. The psalmist was inspired when he wrote, "My soul thirsts for God, for the living God" (Psa. 42:2), and "The Lord will watch over your coming and going both now and forevermore" (Psa. 121:8). Verily, the ever-living God watches over us and walks with us. "Commit your life to the Lord; trust in him and he will act" (Psa. 37:5.) Believing firmly that God is ever living and always watching over me released me from turmoil and filled my heart with elation.

God is love. "This is how God showed his love among us: He sent his one and only Son into the world that we might live through him" (I John 4:9). Through Jesus Christ, God declared, "All that the Father gives me will come to me, and whoever comes to me I will never drive away" (John 6:37). After quiet meditation, and profound contemplation and deliberation, I resolved to secure the anchor of my spirit staunchly and immediately in my submission to God's omnipotent power. Thus, my soul could truly taste that God is good, and my heart filled with joy, peace, and consolation.

With regard to our difficulty in bearing the trials of pain and suffering, I believe our loving God is earnest in solving the problems of his children. As it was written, "No temptation has seized you except what is common to man. And God is faithful; he will not let you be tempted beyond what you can bear. But when you are tempted, he will also provide a way out so that you can stand up under it" (I Cor. 10:13). Take the tumultuous years of the Cultural Revolution in China. I was like a leaf or a wretched lone craft in a raging sea. Eventually, I broke through the waves of obstacles and passed into safety. That was a God-given, invaluable spiritual experience.

The proper attitude towards pain and suffering is a firm faith that "He who did not spare his own Son, but gave him up for us all—how will he not also, along with him, graciously give us all things?" (Rom. 8:32). My injury came out of God's love for me. He wanted to mould me according to his plan, so that I could possess a pure heart. As it is written in Hebrews 12:10, "Our fathers disciplined us for a little while as they thought best; but God disciplines us for our good, that we may share in his holiness."

On a deeper level, let us consider the fact that Christ also suffered in order to save us. Jesus is "now crowned with glory and honour because he suffered death, so that by the grace of God he might taste death for everyone" (Heb. 2:9). We are all sinners. We suffer a little according to God's plan, and we should be acquiescent. The prophet Samuel tells us, "To obey is better than sacrifice, and to heed is better than the fat of rams" (I Sam. 15:22). We should follow Christ's example: "And being found in appearance as a man, he humbled himself and became obedient to death—even death on a cross" (Phil. 2:8).

I am grateful to God for the advanced technological treatment I received and the sustained rehabilitation program available to me so that I was able to recover to a definite degree. However, I still need others to take care of me in my daily life and I feel I am teetering on the brink of being disabled. Even so, I am constantly contented, optimistic and easy going, due to the power of prayer from my Christian brothers and sisters. In fact, I feel no different from a child who has just been weaned, balanced and tranquil within. May all my brothers and sisters in Christ be healthy, both in body and in spirit, and their love for God and fellow humans increase day by day!

## 46. Receiving My Second Honour

While I was undergoing treatment in North York General Hospital, I received an invitation from Trinity College, Toronto, to attend a convocation on May 14, 1991, and receive an honourary Doctorate of Divinity degree. At that time, I was seriously ill and could not possibly attend the ceremony in person. Later, the college granted permission for my sister Rita to receive the honour on my behalf. The day after the convocation, Rita brought the diploma to my bedside for me to see. I was overjoyed and excited, and filled with praise and thanksgiving. How often do these exceptional events happen in one's life? The memory of them is dearly cherished.

*The Rev. Dr. Florence Li Tim-Oi was called back to heaven, in her sleep, on February 26, 1992.*

# In Remembrance of My Sister, Tim-Oi, November 26, 1992

## Rita K. Lee-Chui

✢ ✢ ✢

My sister departed from this world on February 26, 1992, at the age of eighty-five. The night before, I had sat by her bedside and conversed with her until around midnight. She enjoyed the long conversation and took an interest in all the subjects we talked about. She recalled some small matters that should have been done but were yet undone, and she charged me to take action to clear them up. When I left her, I advised her to retire as soon as possible, and I said good night. I went back to my own apartment. (Tim-Oi lived on the second floor and I live with my husband, Siu-Ting, on the seventh floor.)

At nine o'clock the following morning, the Chinese woman who had been looking after my sister knocked at her door. When Tim-Oi did not come to open it, she suspected something was wrong. She rushed up to our apartment to inform us about the situation; my husband, who was already up and dressed, immediately went with her to open my sister's door and dashed into Tim-Oi's bedroom. They found her in bed, resting as in a deep slumber.

My husband quickly phoned me, and I, in turn, called Dr. Arnold Wong by phone, begging him to come and examine my sister. Dr. Wong reached my sister's bedside before I did, and upon seeing me, declared that my sister's heart had stopped beating several hours before. At that moment, I found it difficult to accept the fact that my sister had died, as her death seemed to have occurred rather suddenly. I felt terribly upset. I phoned the Rev. Edmund Der to report my sister's death. Afterwards, I got in touch with my brother and other close relatives, and requested that they come to help me with the planning of Tim-Oi's funeral.

The last conversation I had with my sister was on the night of February 25. Although she had been suffering from a serious itch over the previous two weeks, she still had enthusiasm for long chats with me. Therefore, I did not feel uncomfortable that night; I had no premonition whatsoever of her fast approach to the end of her life's journey. It did not occur to me that my sister would leave me forever a few hours after I had left her side.

Before Tim-Oi's death, Siu-Ting and I had been away from Canada on holiday for over three months. I had phoned a number of times from Hong Kong and also Vancouver to enquire after her health and to make sure that the arrangements I had made for her material needs were being properly carried out. I had also given special instructions to my brother and a niece to take good care of Tim-Oi so that I might not have serious worries about her during my travels.

What great rejoicing we had when my husband and I returned to Toronto on February 16, 1992, to find ourselves in reunion with Tim-Oi! Alas, it was quite beyond our expectations that, a mere ten days after our reunion, my sister would leave us. It hurts me to remember those ten precious days, which were all too short. I felt great remorse after her death and reproached myself for not having come back to Toronto sooner. I might have had more time to take care of my sister personally and to give her my company.

Since my sister's passing, I have had frequent reminiscences of the childhood and adolescent days that the eight children of our family spent together, in a warm home atmosphere, full of animation. However, the time came for some of us to go to the university, and we sisters and brothers had to separate from one another. Since then it has not been easy for us to have a complete reunion.

I will never forget the school years I spent in Hong Kong with Tim-Oi, my fourth brother, and my sixth brother. We lived together in a rented place. Tim-Oi was the general house-keeping manager, and my two brothers and I were responsible for shopping and odd chores. Tim-Oi was a good leader, and she loved us dearly. Every Sunday, she went with us to attend service at St Paul's Church. She also took us to participate in the Christmas and Easter activities.

When I was a little girl, I was very active and naughty (as I was the youngest of the three girls). Sometimes I did things to offend Tim-Oi; fortunately, she did not lodge any complaint with our parents, or else I might have received punishment from them. Tim-Oi was of a magnanimous nature, and she always dispensed me from the offences I had committed against her. Today, when I think of all this, I feel sorry for not having done enough to pay her back for the kindness and great affection she had for me.

I thank God whole-heartedly for giving my sister and me the opportunity to see each other again in Canada at the end of 1981. This was after thirty-three years of separation. Furthermore, I thank God for making it possible for me to move from Geneva to Toronto and to find a suitable place in which my sister and I could spend our retirement together. During those happy years, we discussed the different issues and experiences we had acquired over the thirty-odd years we had been apart. At times, our different viewpoints on certain issues gave rise to unpleasant debates or controversy. However, such debates were of mutual benefit, because through them there emerged a better understanding between my sister and myself, and a growing affection for each other.

Many aspects of the life of this unusual sister of mine deserve to be remembered. Since her youth, Tim-Oi had proven to be an ambitious person; I would say that she was a woman ahead of her time. In all that she did—be it an ordinary job or an important task—she would give her best. She never shrank from any hardship. She was intent on learning and improving herself. Other outstanding qualities were her patience, modesty, magnanimity, and willingness to forgive those who trespassed against her.

In spite of her failing eyesight in her later years, my sister tried hard to keep abreast of the times by regularly reading books, journals, and daily newspapers. She strictly observed her daily devotion. She kept her diary almost without interruption; on some days more details were written down than on others. The last entry in her diary was dated February 24, 1992, only two days before she passed away. It was a very brief entry, mentioning the video tapes "Return to Hepu—Li Tim-Oi Goes Home" and the "Wedding of Rita and Siu-Ting Chui." Tim-Oi had viewed these tapes happily in the company of Siu-Ting, me, and Yee-Mei (our second sister-in-law).

I had and still have deep affection and great respect for my sister; I had wanted her to be a centenarian. It causes me great pain to think that she has left us. Nevertheless, I know very well that my sister had, during more than half a century, devoted herself to Christian work with a singleness of heart, and expended all the ability with which God had endowed her. She was thus able to serve the church, to work for the service of others, to bear witness for Christ, and to preach the gospel so as to lead people to follow Jesus.

Therefore, as regards to my sister's passing, I reminisce with gratitude and thankfulness to God. The Lord's timing is mysterious. When Tim-Oi was very ill and physically exhausted, He decided to save her from further pain and suffering and received her back into His embrace—in a most peaceful and serene manner. Hence, my sister was guaranteed eternal rest and perpetual joy. When I think of this, my heart is filled with peace and consolation. I have to thank God for His grace and to praise Him!

# A Sermon Preached in St Matthew's and St John's, Toronto, at the Golden Jubilee of the Ordination of Florence Li Tim-Oi, January 25, 1994

## Archbishop Ted Scott

✣ ✣ ✣

O God, for as much as without you, we are not able to please you, mercifully grant that in this and all things that your Holy Spirit may direct and rule our hearts and minds through Jesus Christ. Amen.

It is a very great honour and privilege to have been asked to share in this special service marking the fiftieth anniversary of the ordination to the priesthood of Li Tim-Oi, the first woman to be ordained priest within the Anglican Communion.

It is a particularly special day for me, as it happens to be the twenty-eighth anniversary of my consecration as a bishop and the twenty-third anniversary of my installation as Primate of the Anglican Church of Canada. I can think of no better way to celebrate those events than by thinking about the contribution that Li Tim-Oi, who was ordained to the priesthood in the Church of God fifty years ago, has made not only to the Anglican Communion but to the worldwide church. It is also good that this event is being celebrated by representatives of a wide range of ethnic groups—Florence would have wanted this. She would also be glad that it takes the form of a con-celebration in which both men and women priests are celebrants. Florence would have wanted this also. Again, on a personal level, I am delighted that Bishop Arthur Brown is one of the celebrants because as rector of St Michael's and All Angels he con-celebrated with me and David Woeller on the first Sunday after I was elected Primate.

About twelve years ago, on the last official visit I made as Primate to the United States, I was to be interviewed for both radio and television and had been sent a note indicating some of the questions I would be asked. (They never tell you *all* the questions planned for such interviews!) One of the questions was quite unexpected, and I was very glad I had been warned about it: "Who would you feel were the ten persons who have most influenced your life as a person and as a Bishop?" I had to think hard about that question—it was not one I had ever been asked before. After giving it some thought, I made a list of persons whom I knew had influenced me deeply, and then reviewed it thoughtfully on several occasions. I finally whittled it down to ten.

When I showed the final list to some friends before leaving for the United States, they pointed out several things I had not noticed. In the group of ten there were five different ethnic groups represented and four different skin colours. It consisted of six women and four men. Among the women was Florence Li Tim-Oi.

I had heard of Florence, as I came to know her, long before I actually met her. In the 1960s, I served as the staff person of the National Committee on the Role of Women in the Church, and it was in that capacity that I first learned of her existence.

When, as a church, we began to explore the possibility of the ordination of women to the diaconate and the priesthood in the Anglican Church of Canada, we studied things that had already taken place in our Communion, and in others. It was then that I learned more about Bishop Hall's decision to ordain Florence and of the reactions of the wider Communion to this action. I had many discussions with Bishop Baker (Bishop Hall's successor), and learned more about the circumstances and the consequences of that action in the Diocese of Hong Kong. It was only some years later, after we had met personally, that I learned from her more of the details of what had taken place.

When I was moderator of the World Council of Churches, I had contact with her sister and with other members of her family. Through these contacts I learned that there was now a possibility that Florence might be allowed to leave China and come to Canada, if Canada was prepared to accept her. Contact was established with the Immigration Department and assurance was given that she could come as a sponsored immigrant. Following a number of delays, word was received that she would be accepted and the necessary arrangements for an exit visa from China were finally completed.

When the possibility of her coming had been raised, I initiated contact with the Diocese of Hong Kong about the details of her ordination. By that time we had acted to ordain women to the priesthood in Canada, and I hoped that it would be possible to give her authority to exercise her priesthood in this country. Her sister had indicated that Florence hoped that this might be so. Sure enough, one of the first things she asked when she arrived was whether or not this would be possible, and if so, how long it would be before authority could be given. Her desire to be able to exercise her priesthood was very deep. The first time she celebrated the Eucharist after she received her licence must have been a wonderful experience for her and for all present—I wish I could have been there.

We learned that many of the records of the Diocese of Hong Kong had been destroyed in a fire, including the record of her ordination. This meant that investigations had to be undertaken and sworn affidavits stating that she had been ordained according to the canons of the Diocese of Hong Kong had to be obtained. Without these it would not be possible to give her the necessary authority. At the first meeting of the House of Bishops after the necessary documentation had been secured, I reported her situation to the House, urging that permission be given for her to receive the necessary authority to exercise her priesthood here in Canada. This was granted, if I remember correctly, by a unanimous vote. It was a very joyful occasion for me to convey this information to her, and it was clearly a decision that she welcomed.

Since she was then living in Montreal, Bishop Hollis, the Bishop of Montreal, licensed her to exercise her priesthood. She exercised a wonderful ministry there. When she came to Toronto, she was transferred from the Diocese of Montreal to the Diocese of Toronto just as any other priest would be.

It was when I had the opportunity to talk with her that I learned more about what had actually happened following her ordination. In a sense she had never been officially prevented from exercising her priesthood. When she became aware of the reaction of other parts of the Anglican Communion to her ordination, she realized that Bishop Hall would be under extreme pressure. She had made the personal decision to resign the exercise of her priesthood, believing that this action would be in the best interests of all concerned. The decision was her own—Bishop Hall had never asked her to resign. She had tremendous love and respect for Bishop Hall and for the Anglican Communion. She was very clear in her own mind that she had never given up the "priesthood" bestowed upon her in ordination but had made the decision not to exercise it until she received permission from the Communion to do so. This explains why the permission granted by the Anglican Church of Canada meant so much to her. She remained meticulous in not exercising her priesthood in provinces, such as England, where the decision to ordain women to the priesthood had not yet been made.

Whereas the decision meant that she would not exercise the specialized ministry of a priest, it never prevented her from ministering in a wide variety of ways. I would like to know much more than I do about the time she spent in China, but I do know that she ministered in a wide range of circumstances with very great faithfulness—word of that faithfulness spread far beyond China.

I do not think Florence was ever aware of the tremendous influence she had, both on individual persons and on the church. She influenced me very deeply and I know that she also influenced many leaders of the World Council of Churches. She had a great influence upon the thinking of the church. She modelled faithfulness, and when she was given the authority to do so, she modelled priesthood at its best. Her example led many people struggling with the issue, among them Archbishop Runcie, to move to a more positive stance vis à vis the ordination of women.

Although I had been invited to be present at the Lambeth Conference in 1988 when a celebration was held recognizing her ordination, I was not able to be there. However, I talked with her on several occasions about what that event meant to her. Archbishop Runcie spoke about how he had learned in the course of his travels of the impact she had made wherever she had visited and acknowledged the impact she had made on him and on many within the church.

The Anglican Consultative Council had recognized her tremendous contribution and assisted in the planning of the event at Lambeth. They were involved in the preparation of a video tape on her life and ministry.

Tonight we meet to give honour to Florence. She would be the first to remind us, in her quiet but direct manner, that honour is not given so much by words that are spoken but by showing forth in our lives the same faithfulness that she displayed, and by working for the same goals that she worked for. What were some of these goals?

Under the leading of the spirit, Florence worked hard to break down barriers between human beings of different races and cultures; she worked hard to break down the barriers that exist between the different branches of the Christian community; she worked hard to break down barriers between men and women. But the focus of her life was much more positive than negative—she was more concerned with building up than breaking down. She was concerned about what she believed God meant to be rather than against what was. She worked hard to help a new human community come into being in which people of all races could come together with mutual respect for one another, where men and women could be equal partners, honouring each other and the contribution each could make—seeking to set each other free to grow and develop to their full potential as persons made in the image of God. All these goals she saw as acknowledging, and seeking to give expression to, the kingdom or rule of God.

Two other persons among the ten whom I know have influenced me greatly share many of the same qualities as Florence. One is Nelson Mandela, who spent twenty-eight years in prison because of the race he belonged to, because of the colour of his skin, and because of the unjust laws that shaped the relationships of the society in which he lived. For twenty-eight years every effort was made by those in authority to prevent him from giving the leadership of which he was capable to the people and country he loved and longed to serve so deeply. Both he and Florence endured restrictions that could easily have made them bitter and disillusioned, but both refused to allow the experiences they endured to make them bitter or vindictive. Both of them in the midst of injustice remained committed to their callings, continued to reach out in love and concern, worked to help something better come to be when their freedom was restricted, and continued to so when the restrictions were removed. What tremendous leadership they have both given.

Another is Verna Dozier, a black, retired high school teacher in Washington, D.C. She too lived through the injustices of white racism and refused to allow herself to become bitter. I am deeply grateful to her because I believe she articulated very clearly and simply the kind of vision which inspired Florence Li Tim-Oi, Nelson Mandela, and many others within the Church.

This vision is expressed in her faith about the activity of God. She maintains that God entered human history in Jesus Christ to bring into being a new people, the church, the baptized community. We meet tonight as a gathered expression of that community. This community of which we are members, Verna maintains, is called to change the world—to help come into being a world

> in which every human being knows that he or she is loved and valued; a world in which every human being knows that he or she, because of the gifts of life, of energy, and of talents which each has received, is called to make a contribution to the human community, to the lives of others; a world in which every human being has the right to share in the gifts of creation.

This vision of the world is very different from the realities of the world that Florence Li Tim-Oi experienced and in which she lived her life with such faithfulness, but this is the kind of world for which she worked.

If we would truly honour her, we must commit to helping this kind of world come to be, even as she did.

We can be involved in this task every day of our lives, wherever we may be, under whatever kind of conditions we may find ourselves. Each and every day you and I touch the lives of some other people, as Florence did. Do we help those whose lives we touch to know that they are loved and valued? Do we help them to know that they have a contribution to make? Florence did this for the people whose lives she touched and if we would truly honour her we must do the same for those whose lives we touch. This is our calling, as it was hers. It is a glorious calling! Amen.

# *Thoughts at the First Ordination of Women Priests at St. Mary's Banbury, Oxfordshire, on Sunday, April 17, 1994*

## Christopher Hall

✣ ✣ ✣

Fifty years ago my father was, he said, 99 percent coward, yet he had the courage of his convictions to ordain Li Tim-Oi to be the first woman priest in the Anglican Communion. The *Church Times* was furious: it headlined its report "Bishop in Insurrection," and called my father a "wild man from the woods." In the week following his death thirty-one years later, the *Church Times* printed their analysis of the votes in the dioceses of England. It showed that 65.3 percent of Diocesan Synod voters across the country had opted for ordaining women priests in principle, and 62.5 percent of those who voted wanted it done then. Unwittingly, the *Church Times* printed that report on the back of a generous tribute to my father. There was, I'm sure, laughter in paradise. It has taken a further nineteen years to bring us here this morning; more than fifty years on from that St Paul's Day in 1944. And yet it only took seventeen years from Pentecost, the first Whitsunday, to the Council of Jerusalem for the early church to welcome the gentiles fully into their fellowship.

May I share with you something else that I rediscovered only a few weeks ago? When my father retired in 1966, he was given what was for him a new-fangled invention—a reel-to-reel tape recorder. A spell in hospital gave him the time to try it out, and he began to record a book on priesthood. He never completed it. What he wrote has never been made public until today. In his vision of the priesthood, he saw the admission of Li Tim-Oi and of many others. I would like to be able to play the actual recording to you because the passionate conviction of his voice is part of his message, but the recording is poor and hard to decipher. He describes himself as "a pious old septuagenarian." It was twenty-five years ago, so please forgive him for any lack of inclusive language.

He begins by saying, "Above all things a parson must be a Man of God—a man of God in the sense that every man or woman is a member of God's family, charged with the priesthood of Christ, with being an ambassador for him, and with being his representative—his persona in the world."

And who is the God priests are to impersonate, to represent? The God my father served is the Self-giver, the self-giving Father portrayed in the parable of the prodigal son, the father who is prodigal with himself, going out to give himself to both of his sons. To give, says my father, "to those who are utterly untrustworthy, what you know they are not to be trusted with, is the height of folly, but this is the relationship that God the Self-giver has with Creation. While we were yet in our sins, Christ died for us. He gave himself utterly for all the world without any conditions. God letting the world he had made, break him. God present in the brokenness. God redeeming through the acceptance of brokenness and all the power of love that he pours out all the time. Those who notice and respond and use it become indeed his priests, his representatives, whoever they may be."

He continues: "Perhaps the sun is the best illustration of what this means. The sun after all is one of God's greatest servants in creation. Without the Sun there could have been no human life.... The whole nature of the sun is like our Lord's death upon the cross, an utter self-giving, an utter giving of all that is himself, pouring it out without any thought or question of who is going to be the receiver at the other end, giving it to all men, pouring it out so that it is available to those who, like the earth, have accepted the warmth of the sun, and their side is turned towards it. From that accepted warmth life grows. So man's response to God's self-giving makes possible the fulfilment of God's creation—in the life and work of God and man as fellow-workers together." That is how my father described the eternal nature of God, in which God calls us to share as his representatives—to be his priests—men and women for God.

But my father also urges us not to be backward-looking. He wanted to print Sydney Carter's poem "In the Present Time" at the beginning of that chapter on priesthood. The last line reads, "Shut the Bible up and show me how the Christ you talk about is living now."

On the fortieth anniversary of her ordination, Tim-Oi visited St Margaret's Church in Lewknor, Oxfordshire, where she prayed close to the memorial tablet dedicated to my father on the sanctuary wall. It bears this inscription: "He showed us how the Christ he talked about is living now." That is the role of priesthood, the priesthood to which women as well as men are now ordained, and equally, too, the role of the priesthood to which all believers are called, the priesthood that the warmth of the outpouring love of God has already given to Tim-Oi, the gift of that priesthood. All he did was to give it public expression.

I first remember speaking to Tim-Oi on the phone from Toronto, as we arranged her first visit to England for the celebrations of the fortieth anniversary of her priesting. It was the greatest joy to meet her for the first time during the Exchange of the Peace at the Eucharist in Westminster Abbey. The following Saturday she attended the special service in Sheffield Cathedral, at which I reflected on the story of Cornelius, the first gentile to be baptised. Forty years before, my father had been tempted to rename Tim-Oi "Cornelia," because he saw the close parallel between the first baptised gentile and the first woman priest.

She came back to Bolton with us and preached in the parish church the following morning. Her text must have been a favourite of hers: "Having loved his own, he loved them unto the end." That and the knowledge of her priesthood carried her through all that she endured from the Chinese Red Guards as well as from the church's "purple guards." In the porch after the service, she unbent even the most unbending of parishioners, reaching out to bring them down to her level for a kiss.

Getting to know her for the first time that weekend, I came to the conviction that she was not a woman who just happened to be around at that time and place. God had prepared her for her role in His story.

While revisiting her old parish in China at the age of eighty, she insisted on tackling a pastoral crisis. Bob Browne heard the debate in the next room. Her sister said, "It's not your problem." Tim Oi retorted, "Rita, you no tough guy like me," and off she went down the hotel corridor. In the warmth of God's love, "she showed us how the Christ she talked about is living now." God give us all warmth to be his priests, "to show the world how the Christ we talk about is living now."

# *A Sermon Preached in St Martin-in-the-Fields at the Golden Jubilee of the Ordination of Florence Li Tim-Oi, January 25, 1994*

## Archbishop Donald Coggan

✣ ✣ ✣

Then Peter began: "I now understand how true it is that God has no favourites.... Is anyone prepared to withhold the water of baptism from these persons, who have received the Holy Spirit just as we did?" (Acts 10:34,37)

Those are astonishing words, coming from that old conservative, the man with the big mouth and the big heart and the God-given insight—Peter!

To such a congregation as this, there is no need to re-tell the story of Peter and that godly gentile, Cornelius, whose prayers had been heard by God and whose alms spoke for him. Godly though Cornelius was, the idea of eating with him was repellent to Peter—it just was not done. To us, perhaps, the incident might appear trivial. But behind it lay a fundamental issue. Was Christianity to be a branch of the Jewish faith, or was it to be open to all? How does one enter into fellowship with God? Justification by grace through faith—Peter saw it—and dared! "I now understand how true it is that God has no favourites.... Is anyone prepared to withhold the water of baptism from these persons, who have received the Holy Spirit just as we did?" The door was open. The ground was level. Race, sex, status, these were irrelevant.

To this congregation, there is no need to elaborate on the parallel between that incident and the one we celebrate today—the fiftieth anniversary of the ordination of Florence Li-Tim Oi.

Two figures are uppermost in our minds and in our thanksgivings today. First is Bishop Ronald Hall of Hong Kong, or "R.O." as he was known to his friends. We salute his memory. He was no hot-head who thoughtlessly dismissed matters of church order. The step he took in ordaining Florence Li-Tim Oi as priest cost him much. He wrote to Reinhold Niebuhr, "I'm 99 percent coward and hate disapproval from anybody." We may doubt his figure, but we take his point. It was only after a day spent at the home of friends, alone and in prayer, that he took the step that he did. He could do no other, unless he was to betray what seemed to him to be the mind of God.

We can argue the rightness or the wrongness of his decision, but the principle of the Peter and Cornelius story is weighty. The Abbé of Tourville wrote: "In every age, God has scattered forerunners in the world. They are those who are ahead of their time and whose personal action is based on an inward knowledge of that which is yet to come." These forerunners "feel themselves to be strangers in a foreign land." R.O. knew what it was to be lonely.

The second figure uppermost in our minds is Florence Li Tim-Oi. That gallant little lady was no fool. Ordained deaconess at the age of thirty-five (having passed the examinations of a full theological course with honours), she spent two years in a large Hong Kong parish. In Macau, she took charge of a new refugee congregation that consisted of schoolmasters, university lecturers, students, people in business, and those holding government posts. She held that congregation. She was a woman of culture and ability—a godly woman.

Fifty years ago today, Bishop Ronald Hall ordained her priest in the Church of God. The controversy this act produced in the Anglican Communion need not now detain us. It was so severe that Florence felt it right to surrender her licence (though not her Orders) as a priest, and to serve again as a deaconess in the Chinese Church. Lesser souls, smarting under such "loss of face," might well have given up church work. Not she. She put church before self. She showed true humility, in obedience to Him who came not to be served but to serve. Thus she showed her greatness.

Many of us recall the service in Westminster Abbey ten years ago, when, in her presence, we met to thank God. Surely, her spirit is with us today—rejoicing!

We have looked at two lovely characters: "R.O.," with his passion for truth; Li Tim-Oi, with her passion for service and for building up the Body of Christ. It has been a wholesome exercise—"thanks be to God." But what is to be the outcome of this service? "A good time was had by all"? Just that and no more? God forbid.

We look forward to the ordination of women as priests in a few weeks time. For it, many here have laboured long and hard. At last! I want you to help these women of God. They will be the focus of attention by the media. The cameras will be on them. No doubt the things that matter least will be most highlighted by the media: "Who will be first? What will they wear?" What can *we* do?

Shortly before the Lambeth Conference of 1988, I lunched with the Bishop of Washington. The consecration of bishops in the American church was under much discussion. I told the Bishop that I hoped it would not happen before the Conference, for that would exacerbate the debate and damage the cause. But it seemed to me to present the American church with a great opportunity. The consecration of the first woman bishop would give their church a unique opportunity to choose such women as were, not necessarily great organisers, nor even (though they would be needed) great scholars, but *holy* women, women who reflected the beauty of Jesus. Go for holiness!

I want to see this congregation turned into a body of people who will pray daily for the women who are to be ordained—women who will reflect the passion for truth of R.O., women who will reflect the passion of Li Tim-Oi for service and building up the Body of Christ. But above all, women who will bring to the Church of God such an infusion of holiness that some of the darkness we men have brought to the church may be healed by their radiance; some of the cockiness we men have brought to the church may be healed by their humility; some of the wounds we men have inflicted on the church may be healed by their gentleness.

We shall welcome them with warmth.
We shall pray for them with diligence.
God bless them.